VIOLENT PLANET

by Philip Steele, Neil Morris and Nicola Barber

North American edition copyright © ticktock Entertainment Ltd 2008
First published in North America in 2008 by ticktock Media Ltd,
Unit 2, Orchard Business Centre, North Farm Road,
Tunbridge Wells, Kent TN2 3XF, UK

ISBN: 978 1 84696 813 6
Printed in China

Picture credits (t=top; b=bottom; c=center; l=left; r=right):
AKG 12c & 12br. Ancient Art & Architecture 37cr, 37tr, 60bl, 61tr, 73tr, 85br. Ann Ronan/Image Select 21br, 74tl, 75b, 80tl, 87br, 88tl.
Anthony Blake Photo Library 36br. Associated Press 76br, 77br. The British Museum 12tl. CFCL/Image Select 15bl. Colorific 5t, 5b, 42/43
(main pic), 48tl, 60/61 (main pic), 70bl, 72br, 78/79b, 87bl, 94bl, 94/95 (main pic), 97tr, 98cr, 103br, 104br, 107tr, 109tr, 113t,
114tl, 114c, 115tl, 114/115 (main pic), 116cl, 117b, 116/117t, 120c, 125b. Corbis 6tl, 7tr, 8tl, 9tr, 12tl, 46tl, 46/47 (main pic), 52c,
55b, 56tl, 56/57t, 57br, 58tl, 65br, 65tl, 64/65b, 71bl, 74bl, 85c, 86tl, 95cl, 109cr, 110/111 (main pic), 112/113 (main pic), 117tr,
119cb, 122/123 (main pic). e.t.archive 68c, 73b, 92bl, 120tl. FPG 76/77b, 86/87bl. G Allen 90/91b. Giraudon 12bl, 13br, 15cr. Image
Select 46bl, 48br, 51br, 54bl, 54tl, 60tl, 60/61cb. Images 19cr, 33tr. Kobal 84t. Mary Evans Picture Library 15tr, 49br, 123tr. NASA 14tl.
National Geographic Society 50br, 52/53br, 53tr, 56b, 57cr, 64/65 (main pic), 76tr, 82cr, 100/101t, 114bl. Controller of HMSO © Crown
Copyright; 90cl. NHPA 78br, 78/79t. Oxford Scientific Films 2, 14b, 10tl, 12/13 (main pic), 18br, 29cr, 29bl, 32tl, 40bc, 40/41 (main
pic), 50tl, 92/93cb, 110tl. Planet Earth 10c, 17cr, 20c, 22/23b, 22b, 25tr, 26/27t, 28tr, 28bl, 31br, 34cr, 36/37 (main pic), 54/55
(main pic), 58b 80/81 (main pic), 91tr 92cl, 94/95cb, 104tl, 104/105 (main pic), 106/107b, 108tl, 110bl, 110/111b. Popperfoto OBC,
7br, 9br, 58/59 (main pic), 42br, 58cl, 58/59 (main pic), 70/71t, 96bl, 100cl, 101br, 101tr, 106bl, 108bl, 118cl, 118/119 (main pic).
Rex Features 16b, 21cr, 22t, 24/25 (main pic), 25bl, 25br, 27cb, 26tl, 26bl, 26br, 26bl, 31c, 33cl, 36tl, 59cl, 61br, 68tl, 74/75tl, 80cr,
82tl, 93bc, 92tl, 95br, 95tr, 106/107t, 108/109 (main pic). Ronald Grant Archive 72bl. Science & Society 47tr. Science Photo Library 5c,
14/15t, 16cl, 16t, 11tr, 11c, 18/19 (main pic), 20/21 (main pic), 20tl, 29tr, 31tr, 34bl, 35br, 36cl, 38/39t, 38cb, 38cl, 39br, 39bl, 40bl,
12cb, 42l, 44/45 (main pic), 48/49 (main pic), 48/49c, 50/51 (main pic), 62/63 (main pic), 62bl, 63tr, 63br, 64bl, 66cl, 66tl, 66/67t,
67br,70cr, 84/85, 88/89 (main pic), 89cb, 97br, 102tl, 102/103t, 121bl, 125t. Shutterstock OFC. Spectrum Colour Library 74bl, 78tl,
78cl, 122cb, 123cr, 122/123b. Still Pictures 28br, 28/29t, 70tl, 72/73t, 76c, 86/87tr, 87cr, 90/91 (main pic), 104bl, 105cb, 118/119b.
The Stock Market 12/13t. Telegraph Colour Library 1, 4b, 6/7, 8/9 (main pic),16/17t, 17br, 23c, 44/45cb, 68b, 83br 85tr, 89cr,
98/99t, 120/121 (main pic). Tony Hobbs 89br. Tony Stone 20b, 22cr, 30/31 (main pic), 32b, 32/33t, 34/35 (main pic), 42tl, 76/77t,
82/83 (main pic), 96tl, 96/97 (main pic), 98/99t, 99b, 107br.

CONTENTS

INTRODUCTION

About this Book 4
The Violent Earth 6
Plate Tectonics 8
Fault Lines 10

VOLCANOES

The Gates of Hell 12
Mountains of Doom 14
From the Depths 16
Inside the Volcano 18
Signs and Warnings 20
Blowing its Top 22
Clouds of Death 24
Disaster Zone 26
Aftermath 28
Tell-tale Rocks 30
Life after Lava 32
Volcano Science 34
Volcanoes of the Past 36
Volcanoes in Space 38

EARTHQUAKES

What is an Earthquake? 40
San Andreas Fault 42
Seismic Waves 44
Measurement 46
Lisbon, 1755 48
Tsunamis 50
Landslides & Mudflows 52
Manmade Quakes 54
Mexico City, 1985 56
Honshu, Japan 58
Earthquakes of the Past 60
Predicting Earthquakes 62
Looking to the Future 64

HURRICANES & TORNADOES

What is a Hurricane? 66
Where in the World? 68
Atlantic Hurricanes 70
Big Winds of the Pacific 72
The Indian Ocean 74
Biggest Storms 76
Destroying Darwin 78
What is a Tornado? 80
Tornado Alley 82
Amazing Whirling Winds 84
Safety Precautions 86
Weather Watch 88
The World's Weather 90
El Niño 92
Looking to the Future 94

FIRE & FLOOD

The Uncontrollable Elements 96
Fires — Why do they Happen? 98
Floods — Why do they Happen? 100
Signs & Warnings 102
Extreme Weather 104
Hot Spots 106
Fighting a Wildfire 108
After a Fire 110
Prevention & science: Fire 112
Wet Spots 114
Living with the Threat 116
After a Flood 118
Prevention & Science: Floods 120
Uncovering the Past 122

Glossary 124
Index 126

Most of the time, ours is a beautiful and peaceful planet—where humans introduce the only commotion! But now and again, and sometimes without any warning, nature really flares up and makes itself visible. Commonly called "natural disasters"— volcanoes, earthquakes, tsunamis, hurricanes, tornadoes, fires, and floods can have a devastating impact on landscape and on people's lives.

ABOUT THIS BOOK

The world beneath our feet seems solid, but it is constantly on the move. Countries and seas lie on massive tectonic plates which are slowly moving apart in some places and being crushed together in others. The plates move at less than an inch a year, but the tremendous forces involved mean the consequences are hugely destructive. Earthquakes and volcanoes are both caused by shifts in tectonic plates. These phenomena can trigger fires and floods that cause even more destruction than the original natural disaster.

VOLCANOES

Imagine being witness to the terrifying yet breathtaking sight of a volcano erupting! One of the most exciting forces of nature to behold, volcanoes in action are also one of the most deadly. Those unfortunate people whose homes happen to lie near an active volcano will rarely have much, if any, time to escape the river of scorching lava, ash, soot, and smoke that accompany the spectacle. Read about the most explosive natural phenomena the Earth is capable of producing.

EARTHQUAKES

What exactly is an earthquake and what causes one to happen? The thought of the earth rumbling and shaking might seem like something that might not have too much devastating impact on the Earth, but the fact is that some quakes have had awful and catastrophic effects. Learn about the biggest earthquakes to have rocked the Earth and how they have impacted on life and nature.

HURRICANES & TORNADOES

Do you love wrapping up warm in your bed while a storm is raging outside... or are you more the type who will hide under the bed until its over? If it was a tornado or hurricane that was gathering force outside your window, you wouldn't have much chance to make up your mind! Learn about these staggering freak winds that are capable of uprooting houses and cars, and about the communities that live in constant fear of them.

FIRE & FLOOD

Fire and water: both are elements that are essential to human survival, yet when we have too much of one or the other at one time, the result can be utterly disastrous. Discover how severely communities have suffered during and after floods and fires. Many communities are more likely to face these threats—find out why and what they can do when it happens.

NATURAL DISASTER HOTSPOTS

Volcanoes
Japan
Western America
New Zealand

Tornadoes
North America
Europe
East Asia
Australia

Hurricanes
USA
Caribbean
Bangladesh
South America

Earthquakes
China
USA
Mexico
Japan

Bushfires
Southeast Australia
Southeast Asia
Western USA
Southern France

Floods
Bangladesh
India
Mississippi, USA
Venice, Italy

THE VIOLENT EARTH

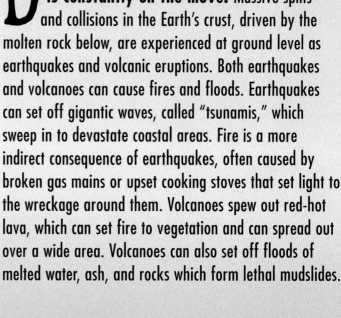

SAN FRANCISCO, 1906

The people of San Francisco are used to tremors shaking the ground beneath their feet. But the quake that shook people awake on the morning of April 18, 1906 was more than a tremor. It lasted for minutes and caused buildings to collapse across the city. As the bewildered people fled their homes and started to take in their unfamiliar surroundings a new threat became apparent—fires started by innumerable upset stoves, broken electric wires and ruptured gas mains. The water supplies used to fight fire had been ruptured in the earthquake, and there was little that people could do but watch their city burn for three days and two nights.

Deep down beneath your feet, the Earth is constantly on the move. Massive splits and collisions in the Earth's crust, driven by the molten rock below, are experienced at ground level as earthquakes and volcanic eruptions. Both earthquakes and volcanoes can cause fires and floods. Earthquakes can set off gigantic waves, called "tsunamis," which sweep in to devastate coastal areas. Fire is a more indirect consequence of earthquakes, often caused by broken gas mains or upset cooking stoves that set light to the wreckage around them. Volcanoes spew out red-hot lava, which can set fire to vegetation and can spread out over a wide area. Volcanoes can also set off floods of melted water, ash, and rocks which form lethal mudslides.

ALASKA, 1964

Twisted and broken railway tracks lie along the coast of Alaska, USA, the result of a huge earthquake that hit Alaska on March 27 1964. The movement of the earth devastated the landscape along the coast of Alaska. Half an hour after the earthquake, the first of several tsunamis hit the coast. These massive waves were over 26 feet (8 m) high as they hit the stricken coastline. The tsunamis swept down the coastline as far as northern California.

MUDFLOW MENACE

The city of Seattle in northwestern USA is overlooked by Mount Rainier, one of the many volcanoes in the Cascade chain. The city and other towns nearer the volcano are all built on the remains of mudflows that once poured out of the volcano as it erupted. These mudflows are called lahar. They happen when ash and rock from an erupting volcano mix with melting ice from glaciers on the volcano to form a mass of mud that can move at terrifying speed.

FIRE & ICE

When the Icelandic volcano Grimsvötn began to erupt in autumn 1996, scientists across the world became very excited. This was an unusual eruption because Grimsvötn just happens to lie under a huge icecap called Vatnajökull. As the heat of the eruption melted the ice above, everyone waited for the promised deluge. At the beginning of November the water finally broke through, surging for 30 miles (48 km) beneath the ice before emerging from beneath the icecap. The power of the flood left the floodplain along the south coast of Iceland littered with gigantic rocks and chunks of ice 30 feet (9 m) high. This type of flood is called a jökulhlaup, an Icelandic word meaning "glacier flood."

PLATE TECTONICS

We often say that something is as solid as rock. In reality, the Earth's crust is cracked, like a fragile eggshell. The cracked sections, called tectonic plates, are supported by the oozing, soft rocks of the mantle. The unstable borders between the plates are known as "rings of fire." These are danger zones for both earthquakes and volcanoes. The convection currents in the mantle make the plates move very slowly. Over time, they have caused the continents to drift apart. Where plates move apart beneath an ocean, a rift forms in the sea bed. Magma wells up to form new crust, creating a ridge of undersea mountains on either side of the crack.

Smoke pours through vents called fumaroles, in Hawaii Volcanoes National Park. The Hawaiian islands are a group of submarine volcanoes which have not grown up on a plate boundary, but on a "hot spot" in the Earth's crust. Hot spots mark areas of great activity in the mantle, where magma punches its way through a tectonic plate.

Lava flows create new rock to fill the gaps, and heat up the sea water. Along cracks called vents, chimneys of minerals build up, spouting out gases which bubble up through the water.

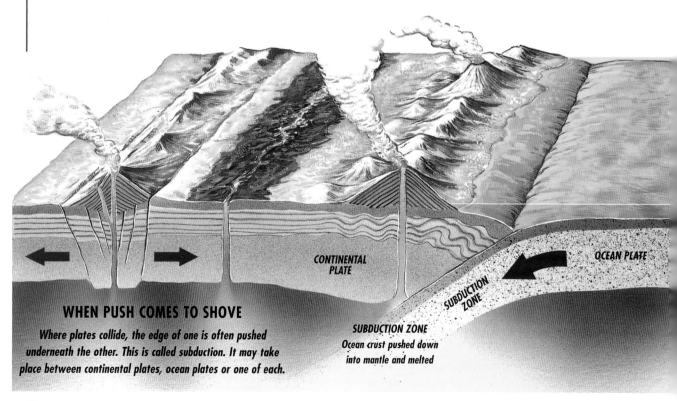

CONTINENTAL PLATE

OCEAN PLATE

SUBDUCTION ZONE

WHEN PUSH COMES TO SHOVE

Where plates collide, the edge of one is often pushed underneath the other. This is called subduction. It may take place between continental plates, ocean plates or one of each.

SUBDUCTION ZONE
Ocean crust pushed down into mantle and melted

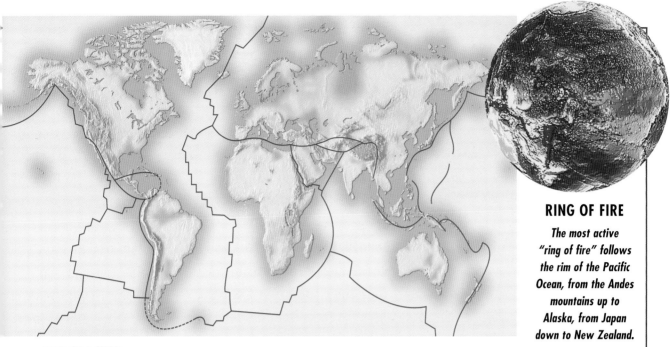

RING OF FIRE

The most active "ring of fire" follows the rim of the Pacific Ocean, from the Andes mountains up to Alaska, from Japan down to New Zealand.

THE CRACKED PLANET

This map shows the plate boundaries. Most of the world's earthquakes and volcanoes are located along these edges. The divides in the ocean floor are called spreading ridges. Beneath the Atlantic Ocean, the sea bed is moving apart at a rate of about ¾ inch (2 cm) each year. Eastern parts of the Pacific sea bed are opening up at about 8 inches (20 cm) per year.

Volcanic activity beneath the sea bed, off the coast of Iceland, created a new island called Surtsey between 1963 and 1966. The new island was named after Surt, who had been lord over the land of fire giants in ancient Norse mythology.

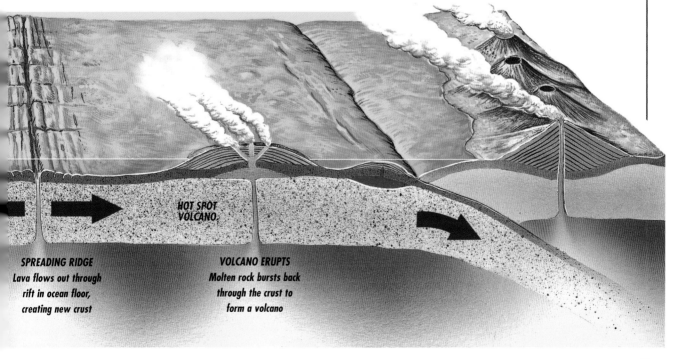

SPREADING RIDGE
Lava flows out through rift in ocean floor, creating new crust

HOT SPOT VOLCANO.

VOLCANO ERUPTS
Molten rock bursts back through the crust to form a volcano

FAULT LINES

As the plates that make up the Earth's crust move and jostle together, they put rocks under such great strain that they sometimes crack. The places where the rocks crack are called faults, and the lines the cracks create are known as fault lines. Large fault lines may go deep into underground rocks and stretch along whole continents. The world's biggest fault lines, like volcanoes and earthquakes, are found near the edges of plates. Some large faults split open the ground when they move, and others push areas of land up or cause it to sink. After an earthquake, when energy has been released, the rock masses on either side of the fault are locked together in new positions. The stresses and strains that caused the original earthquake often begin again and go on building up, until eventually they cause another quake.

Clear evidence of a horizontal fault can be seen from the road marking in this photograph (near Landers, California, in 1992). Earthquakes along horizontal faults have a devastating effect on buildings and other structures, and they are common in California, China, and Turkey.

On the island of Iceland, a large open crack marks the spot where the eastern edge of the North American Plate (on the left in the photograph) meets the western edge of the Eurasian Plate (on the right). The two plates are moving apart at a rate of about 1 inch (2.5 cm) a year, at the same time widening the Atlantic Ocean by the same amount.

GREAT RIFT VALLEY

All the way from the Red Sea to Mozambique, an immense system of faults cuts deep across the face of East Africa. In parts, the Great Rift Valley is up to 62 miles (100 km) wide. It has some of Africa's most spectacular scenery, including lakes and volcanoes. Movements of the African and Somali Plates have formed most parts of the valley, pulling apart the land. In Kenya, this has been going on for millions of years.

NORMAL FAULT

REVERSE FAULT

HORIZONTAL FAULT

DIFFERENT FAULTS

There are different types of faults, depending on the movement of the rocks, and they fall into three main groups. A "normal" fault is caused when tension in the Earth's crust pulls two blocks of rock apart, so that one block slips down along the fault plane.

When the tension pushes two blocks of rock together, one of the blocks is forced to move up the fault plane and form a "reverse" fault.
"Horizontal" faults form when blocks of rock slide past each other sideways.

THE GATES OF HELL

The ground begins to shake and rumble. Mountain peaks are blasted apart. The sky turns dark and lightning forks and flashes. The air becomes poisonous, stinking, choking. Long ago, terrified human beings believed that volcanoes were the work of angry gods or goddesses, of giants or evil spirits. Some believed that volcanoes were gateways to hell. Sometimes human sacrifices were thrown into the crater, to appease the gods. It was not until the 1900s that scientists such as Alfred Wegener began to understand the structure of the Earth's thin outer layer, or crust. Scientists are still learning the truth about volcanoes today—and it really is stranger than fiction.

On the island of Hawaii, there is an ancient custom of making offerings of berries to Pele, the Polynesian volcano goddess. Pele is also known as Hina-Ai-Malama, "she who eats the Moon."

GREEK FIRE

Some ancient thinkers tried to work out how volcanoes might be caused if they weren't the work of gods. The Greek philosopher Aristotle (384-322 BCE) believed that the Earth was honeycombed with caverns, which sucked in the winds. These were heated by great fires and then pushed out again, creating volcanoes.

THE DEVIL'S DOMINION

Most Christians believed hell to be an underground realm of darkness, fire and glowing embers. The devil himself was said to smell of "brimstone" (sulfur). Ideas like these probably had their origins in people's experience of volcanoes and craters such as Mount Etna. Volcanoes were unknown, terrifying and deadly forces—surely, the work of the devil.

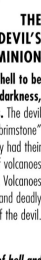

This nightmarish vision of hell and its torments was painted by the Dutch artist Hieronymus Bosch (c. 1450-1516).

VULCAN'S WORKSHOP

Our word "volcano" comes from the name Vulcanus or Vulcan.
From at least 1500 BCE until about 400 CE, the ancient Greeks
worshipped a fire god called Hephaistos. The Romans worshipped the
same god, and called him Vulcanus. The god was said to own great
furnaces, where metals were melted and forged. These were located
inside Mount Etna, on the island of Sicily. Etna still sparks like a
blacksmith's forge today.

*According to one legend, Vulcanus hammered out a magic
shield for the Greek hero Achilles. This could reflect the world
and everything that was in it.*

KRAKATOA, 1883

The volcanic island of Krakatoa, near Java, erupted on August 27 1883. The sound of the explosions could be heard over eight percent of the Earth's surface. At least 36,000 people were killed.

A picture taken from space shows a gaping hole where most of Sumbawa island, in Indonesia, should be. The island was blown apart when Mount Tambora erupted and collapsed in 1815.

VESUVIUS, AD 79
DEATH OF A ROMAN ADMIRAL

In 104 CE, a Roman writer called Pliny the Younger wrote to the historian Tacitus to describe how his uncle, Pliny the Elder (an admiral and man of letters), had died in 79 CE. Pliny the Elder, then aged 56, was stationed with the Roman fleet at Misenum. After lunch on August 24, his sister Plinia pointed out a large cloud rising above the mountains. Pliny hurried to the harbor and ordered the fleet to be launched. He wanted to launch a rescue mission and, as a scientist, take detailed notes of everything he saw. As he approached the danger zone, ash and stones were raining down from Vesuvius. Going ashore at a friend's house at Stabiae, Pliny ate and rested. However, soon Vesuvius was in full spate and thick, choking ash was everywhere. Pliny suffocated on the shore, where his body was found two days later.

AN ANCIENT CRATER

These cliffs on the Greek island of Thíra or Santorini are crater walls, formed by one of the most massive volcanic eruptions ever experienced. In about 1500 BCE, 31 square miles (80 square km) of the island were blasted into oblivion. Clouds of ash and gas drifted over the nearby island of Crete. Thíra erupted again in 1926.

MOUNTAINS OF DOOM

A volcano is an opening in the Earth's crust. Streams of molten rock called lava erupt, or burst out, from the opening. Ashes and rocks may be hurled into the sky. As the lava cools, it hardens and forms new rock. Lava and ash may pile up into a cone, which soon grows into a mountain. Some volcanoes are very violent. Others are more peaceful. Some volcanoes erupt almost all the time, while others only erupt every few hundred or thousand years. Volcanoes which may still erupt are said to be "active." Those which were exhausted long ago are called "extinct." It is all too easy to write off a volcano as extinct — as scientists have found to their cost.

Only two people out of the 30,000 living in St Pierre, on the island of Martinique, survived the catastrophic eruption of Mont Pelée on May 8, 1902.

VESUVIUS THE DESTROYER

Mount Vesuvius rises 3,891 feet (1,186 meters) above the Bay of Naples, in southern Italy.
The height and shape of this volcano has changed many times in history, as the peak has been repeatedly shattered by eruptions and then built up again. The most famous occasion was in 79 CE, when the towns of Pompeii, Oplontis, Stabiae and the seaport of Herculaneum were all destroyed. Vesuvius is a serial killer. It erupted with great force again in 1631, in 1779, 1794, 1822, 1872, 1906, 1929 — and most recently in 1944. This painting is of an 18th-century eruption.

Excavations by archaeologists have uncovered Bronze Age towns on the island of Thíra. This is the site at Akrotíri, where fine buildings decorated with beautiful paintings were destroyed by the eruption in 1500 BCE.

FROM THE DEPTHS

To understand how volcanoes work, we need to take an imaginary journey to the center of our planet. The Earth's center, or core, is about 2,156 miles (3,470 km) thick. It is made up of an inner layer of solid iron and an outer layer of molten iron, cobalt and nickel. Above the core lies about 1,802 miles (2,900 km) of mantle, made up of many different metals. The lower part of this layer is soft and oozy. The upper mantle is solid, but with pockets of hot, molten rock. The Earth's surface, or crust, is up to 37 miles (60 km) thick beneath the continents, but just 3 miles (5 km) thick beneath the sea. The crust is constantly being created and shaped by restless forces deep inside the planet.

THE ROCK FACTORY

We often think of our planet as solid and unchanging. In fact it has been developing ever since it was formed about 4,600 million years ago. The inside of the Earth acts as a giant powerhouse. The red areas in the mantle (yellow) represent rising hot, molten rock, which forms new surface rock, while old surface rock (blue) sinks and is melted down.

CENTRAL HEATING

At the Earth's core, the pressure is awesome and the temperature is about 10,832 °F (6,000 °C). This causes molten rock, called magma, to surge up through the mantle towards the crust. The magma flows driven by this heat are called convection currents. Where magma bursts through the crust, it becomes the building material for oceanic and continental crust.

Earth's core

This computer image shows the movements of the convection currents around the core. The colours show variations in temperature. Dark blue is the coolest at 577 °F (303 °C). Red is the hottest at 2,192 °F (1,200 °C).

An abandoned truck is engulfed by a great flood of lava after an eruption in Hawaii. The forces that shape the Earth's crust are violent and unstoppable. They are necessary for the survival of the planet, but can spell disaster for the humans who live on its surface.

RIVERS OF FIRE

Once magma has burst out into the air or sea, it is called lava. Here, red hot lava forms a long, glowing river on Mauna Loa, Hawaii. As it flows, the molten rock slows, cools and hardens to form new rock.

KILAUEA, HAWAII, 1990

A smouldering stream of lava from Kilauea Crater, in the south of Hawaii, inches its way into town. Lava can erupt at temperatures of up to 2,192 °F (1,200 °C). Even as it cools, it is still more than hot enough to set buildings ablaze and melt roads.

Weak spots in the Earth's crust crack open under the force of the magma swelling up below. Sometimes lava oozes out quietly, sometimes it is spewed up with extreme violence. Here, lava from a volcano in the Hawaiian islands spouts and splutters like boiling, red-hot jam.

VESUVIUS, 1631
DEATH IN DECEMBER

Early in the morning of December 16 1638, the peasants of the Italian region of Campania were herding up their cattle and the priests were in their churches preparing for the festival of Christmas—when Vesuvius erupted again. There had already been months of earth tremors and the crater was gradually filling with lava. At noon, however, two fissures burst open unexpectedly on the southwestern slopes of the volcano. Hot lava flooded out in great rivers. Later that day there were torrential mudslides and new lava flows. Eyewitnesses reported massive falls of ash in the city of Naples. Over 4,000 people perished over the next two days, many in the town of Resina, on the site of ancient Herculaneum.

Sometimes a small crack appears at the side or base of a volcano, leaking gas. Under massive pressure, it may tear open into a long fissure, as happened in the Krafla field in Iceland in 1977. Here we see the 3.2 miles (2 km) fissure releasing large quantities of fluid lava.

ETNA UNPLUGGED

Mount Etna, on the island of Sicily, sits on top of such a large store of rising magma that it is constantly erupting. It rarely has time to build up a large solid plug. This means that the eruptions from its vent are less pressured and less violent than some others.

INSIDE THE VOLCANO

R ed-hot magma from the Earth's upper mantle rises into great reservoirs or chambers inside the Earth's crust. Some of the magma seeps between layers of surface rock, to form sills. Some of it may be trapped inside old fissures, to form dykes. Much of it bursts upwards, to escape through the vents of volcanoes. Repeated eruptions of lava build up steep mountain sides around a powerful central vent. Magma and gases under great pressure also force their way to the surface through secondary vents and fumaroles, leaking gases and steam. The inside of a volcano may be a honeycomb of pipes, vents and fissures. After an eruption, the vents may be plugged as the magma cools and hardens.

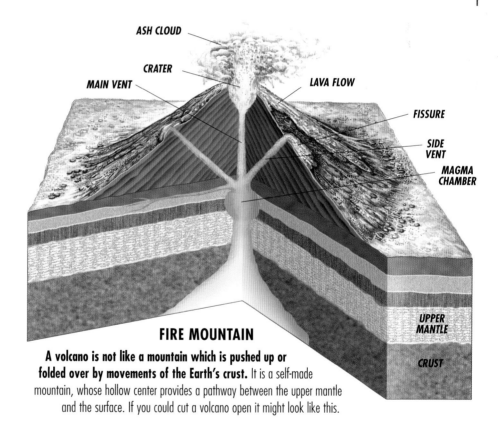

ASH CLOUD

CRATER

MAIN VENT

LAVA FLOW

FISSURE

SIDE VENT

MAGMA CHAMBER

UPPER MANTLE

CRUST

FIRE MOUNTAIN

A volcano is not like a mountain which is pushed up or folded over by movements of the Earth's crust. It is a self-made mountain, whose hollow center provides a pathway between the upper mantle and the surface. If you could cut a volcano open it might look like this.

THE HOLLOW TOOTH

When a violent volcanic eruption blasts the plug from a vent, it shatters the peak and leaves behind a crater. Some craters still connect with a vent to the magma chamber below, while others are blocked off by new plugs of lava and ash. Some of the most impressive craters are called calderas. These are formed when a massive blast empties the magma chamber, causing the volcano to collapse in on itself.

SIGNS & WARNINGS

Volcanic activity is hard to predict. Even scientists are sometimes taken by surprise. However there are warning signs, some of which have been recognized for thousands of years. There is often an increase in seismic activity (earthquakes and tremors) in the region of the volcano. More and more gases pour out of the crater or from side vents, fumaroles and fissures. They may stink of the mineral sulfur, which smells like rotten eggs. There may be rumbling and other strange noises as magma rises up inside the mountain. Sometimes the whole mountainside bulges from the force of magma, causing buildings to be lifted up and the sea to fall back from the shoreline.

• *See page 62-63 for information on predicting earthquakes.*

AN OMINOUS SILENCE

Like its neighbor, Mount Etna, the volcano Mount Stromboli is active most of the time. Its mountain rumbles and grumbles. However, when it falls silent, islanders expect trouble. It often means that rockfalls have blocked the vent and that pressure is building up for a more violent eruption.

SNAKE WATCH

Reports from many parts of the world suggest that the earth tremors and rising ground temperatures, which precede an eruption, drive snakes out of their crevices and burrows.

MOUNT ST HELENS, 1980

"I AM PART OF THE MOUNTAIN"

The date was April 30 1980 and Mount St Helens in Washington State was declared an emergency area. The most dangerous area was the "red zone," to which access was forbidden to all but scientists. Property owners in this zone were evacuated, but one 84-year-old man, named Harry Truman, refused to leave his house by Spirit Lake. On May 12, there was a huge earthquake, but Harry and his 16 cats stayed put. "I am part of the mountain," he told the police patrol. Six days later Harry perished as his home was buried beneath a mound of ash and stone, as the mountain finally collapsed.

WHITE ISLAND, NEW ZEALAND

One measure of volcanic activity is the plume of smoke rising from its summit.
White Island, in New Zealand's Bay of Plenty, offers other clues too. Mud boils and bubbles and whistling jets of steam escape from the ground.

COUNTDOWN: MOUNT ST HELENS

In 1969, American scientists warned that Mount St Helens, a volcano in Washington State, should be carefully watched. From 1975 until 1980, no less than 44 small earthquakes were recorded around the peak. In early 1980, the earthquakes became massive and increasingly frequent. The crater grew and long fissures opened up. The mountainside began to bulge outwards. On May 18 1980, Mount St Helens erupted in a terrifying explosion (below). This infrared photo (left) was taken the day after.

RUN FOR YOUR LIFE!

People flee from the violent eruption of Vesuvius in 1906. A scientific observatory had been opened on the mountain in 1845. Before the volcano erupted, scientists reported tremors, choking gases and a strange buzzing noise from inside the mountain.

KRAKATOA, 1883
SAILING ON THE RIM OF HELL

On the night of August 26 1883, a British sea captain, W. J. Watson of the Charles Bal, was sailing through the Sunda Strait between the islands of Sumatra and Java. As he passed the island of Krakatoa, piles of ash and hot stone showered down on to the wooden deck. The crew, fearing for their lives, shovelled the debris into the sea as fast as it fell. The air stank of sulfur and the sailors could hardly breathe. Lightning forked through the sky and the electrical storm known as "St Elmo's Fire" flickered around the masts. The following morning there was an eerie silence for a time — then at 10 o'clock, the whole island was blasted into the atmosphere with an ear-splitting roar.

THE ROUGH STUFF

Lava rolls down the mountainside. This type is known by a Hawaiian term, aa. It is rough and contains sharp-edged blocks. It is cooler, slower and stickier than other types of lava.

RIPPLES OF ROCK

Black and extremely hot, this lava flow is fast and fluid. It is called by the Hawaiian word pahoehoe. As it cools, it turns into rock with a smooth, rippled surface. Lava which merges under the sea forms rounded blocks called pillows.

SOLID SULPHUR

Volcanic gases contain high levels of sulfur, which solidify as the gases cool to form bright yellow crystals. In some volcanic areas the sulfur is mined, to be used in the manufacture of various products, including rubber and explosives.

BLOWING ITS TOP

A volcanic eruption can blow half a mountain apart. It is an awesome event. The deafening roar from the eruption of Krakatoa in 1883 could be heard on the island of Rodriguez, 2,968 miles (4,776 km) away on the other side of the Indian Ocean. A survivor of the Mount St Helens eruption of 1980 said that it sounded as if the whole mountain had been placed in a giant concrete mixer. Various factors decide just how explosive the eruption will be. Is the vent plugged by cooled magma or debris? If so, the pressure will be greater. Do the volcano's rocks contain water? If so, this can instantly turn into steam, expanding 200 times and smashing through solid rock.

A COLD PLUNGE

On the Hawaiian volcanoes, lava eruptions from the caldera may tower up to 1,640 feet (500 meters). Along fissures, lava may burst out in a long series of lower spouts. It may then start a journey of 19 miles (30 km) or more before cooling. Lava often flows into the sea, where it cools into cliffs of black rock.

Spectators watch in awe as lava pours from the volcanic Galapagos Islands into the Pacific Ocean. Clouds of steam rise from the cold sea water.

HOW THEY BLOW

One eruption may be very different from another. Observers have tried to group volcanoes into various types.

PLINIAN *Gas-rich magma explodes inside the mountain. Cinders, ash and gases are fired up to 19 miles (30 km) in the air.*

PELÉEAN *Gas-rich magma explodes under low pressure. A great cloud of glowing gases, ash and stone rolls down the mountainside like an avalanche.*

HAWAIIAN *After a low-pressure eruption, huge amounts of hot lava flood out and form long flows.*

STROMBOLIAN *Frequent low-pressure eruptions hurl out blocks, blobs of lava and gases.*

VULCANIAN *Periodical higher-pressure explosions hurl out thick lava and very large rocks.*

MT. PELÉE, 1902
BAD ANCHORAGE

On the morning of May 8 1902, the Roraima, a steamship owned by the Quebec Line, was anchored off the port of St Pierre, Martinique. The crew numbered 47 and there were 21 passengers on board. The Chief Officer, a man called Ellery Scott, later gave an account of what happened. He saw a great cloud roll over the town and the sky turned black. The ship lurched and water rose over the deck. The masts and funnel snapped and the rigging came down. The ship caught fire and there were bodies everywhere. Ash and water followed, scalding people and covering them in a cement-like coating. Two hours later, a French ship rescued the 20 or so survivors.

ELECTRIC STORM

As small particles of ash and stone collide and jostle, they crackle with static electricity. Here, lightning plays around Mount Tolbachik, on Russia's Kamchatka peninsula.

India

Krakatoa

Sumatra

FALLOUT ZONE

Java

SOUND ZONE   Australia

THE FALLOUT ZONE

As Krakatoa erupted in 1883, its ash floated down over a vast area of ocean. Some was collected by a ship 994 miles (1,600 km) to the west of the explosion.

MOUNT FUGEN, 1991

This terrifying, smothering cloud of hot gases, ash and smoke is called a pyroclastic flow. Mount Fugen, in the Unzen mountain range in Japan, spewed out lava, ash and hot gases while molten materials rolled down its slopes at 93 mph (150 km/h). Pyroclastic flow can travel at 155 mph (250 km/h).

CLOUDS OF DEATH

During an eruption, clouds of gases such as carbon dioxide and sulfur dioxide escape from the vents. All kinds of materials (known as ejecta) may be hurled high into the air. There are large, solid blocks made of debris or hardened lava; rounded lava "bombs," still molten inside but with a skin on the outside; small stones or pebbles called lapilli. The smallest ejecta are particles the size of a pinhead. These make up a fine ash which drifts like a deadly snowfall. Ash can be carried high into the Earth's atmosphere and stream around the planet in a long trail.

FLYING INTO THE CLOUD

In 1982, Indonesia experienced a powerful Plinian eruption. The Galunggung volcano pumped a mushroom cloud of gas and ash high into the air. Some 75,000 people were evacuated. Whole villages were buried. A British jumbo jet flew into this ash cloud at a height of 36,747 ft (11,200 meters). The dust choked the engines for over 15 minutes and the aircraft only just managed to land.

Islanders from Montserrat, in the Caribbean, grab cardboard boxes to protect themselves as ash falls from the sky. They were later issued with masks. Mount Chance began to erupt in 1995. In the following two years there were pyroclastic flows and an ash cloud which climbed 6 miles (10 km) into the atmosphere.

DISASTER ZONE

People caught up in volcanic eruptions are at risk from many dangers. Earthquakes and eruptions can send shockwaves through the ocean, piling up massive walls of water, called **tsunamis.** Another major risk comes from lava. Earth dams and even bombing by aircraft often fail to divert a strong flow. The molten rock can set forests and buildings ablaze. Gases poison people and ash suffocates them. As the mountainside shakes and collapses, huge avalanches of rock and snow may be released. Snow mixes with soil to create deadly mudslides, called lahars. When Vesuvius erupted in 79 CE, the port of Herculaneum was buried under 43 feet (13 meters) of boiling mud.

• *See page 52-52 for more information on mudslides.*

A TIDE OF MUD

When Nevado del Ruiz erupted in Colombia in 1985, a sea of mud swept through the town of Armero, killing over 23,000 people. To prevent similar disasters, countries such as Japan have built dams and barriers.

A child is rescued from Armero. The best way of saving life is to evacuate people before the eruption. This can be difficult. The volcanoes may be in remote areas and the eruptions may take everyone by surprise.

EMERGENCY RESCUE

Everybody must lend a hand during a major disaster— local people, medical teams, fire-fighters, perhaps the army and airforce too, or international rescue experts. Road and rail links may be destroyed. The eruptions may continue over a long period.

Like a gigantic slag heap, lava creeps over houses on the Icelandic island of Heimaey, after a fissure eruption in 1973.

Ash from the Pinatubo eruption in the Philippines in 1991 clings to the branches of trees. Volcanic eruptions can paralyse towns and cities, close down shops and bring transport to a halt. They often devastate precious forests and destroy crops in the fields, adding the risk of famine to the host of other problems they cause.

HEALTH HAZARDS

Volcanic fallout can cause breathing problems and fire-fighters may suffer burns. Earthquakes can rupture water and gas mains. Water supplies may be poisoned, spreading disease.

ICE AND FIRE

Heimaey is an island off southern Iceland. In 1973 its volcano, Helgafell, was believed to be extinct. But on January 23 a new fissure blew open, near the town of Vestmannaeyjar. The islanders were evacuated to the mainland, but 300 volunteers remained. While a new volcano grew up around the fissure, an enormous lava flow reached the town and threatened to fill the harbor. Many houses were burnt or engulfed. For four months, the islanders sprayed the lava with sea water, hoping to make it cool and solid.

Volcanic soil can be rich and fertile. On the Canary Islands, grape vines are planted in funnel-shaped holes. The porous rock traps the dew, while lava walls provide shelter from the wind.

RABAUL, 1994

Volcanic activity is a creator as well as a destroyer.
At this site in Papua New Guinea, the volcanic islands have been formed by the subduction of one oceanic plate by another.

HEALING THE SCARS

The Mount St Helens eruption of 1980 reduced whole forests to splintered matchwood.
It emptied lakes and filled them with mud and rubble. It blasted out 303 million tons of rock and ash. Yet soon after, plants such as wild lupin and fireweed were pushing up through the layers of ash, and animals were returning to the mountain.

WILDLIFE UNDER THREAT

While some animals soon return to the scene of an eruption, others may find that their habitat has completely disappeared.
In 1998, giant Galapagos tortoises had to be relocated when threatened by a lava flow.

AFTERMATH

The first impression after an eruption is one of total devastation. The hardened lava looks like a lunar landscape. Even the mudslides set as hard as concrete. Peaks have been blown away, and craters have collapsed. Maps of the area need to be redrawn. The release of large amounts of ash into the atmosphere may affect the world's weather for months on end, blocking out the sun. At last, however, life does return to the area. Within 14 years of the Krakatoa eruption in 1883, the fragments which remained as islands had been colonized by no less than 132 species of bird and insect, and by 61 different plant species.

RETURN OF THE PLANTS

How does plant life return to an island after the eruption? Some seeds will be carried there by birds or by the wind. This coconut has floated there on the waves.

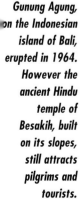

Gunung Agung, on the Indonesian island of Bali, erupted in 1964. However the ancient Hindu temple of Besakih, built on its slopes, still attracts pilgrims and tourists.

THE VALLEY OF 10,000 SMOKES

In 1912, the Novarupta volcano, in remote Alaska, erupted with 10 times the force of Mount St Helens. In its wake it left a new wilderness of ice, rock, and steam.

TELL-TALE ROCKS

Rocky landscapes give us all kinds of clues about the Earth's crust and how it is formed. Rocks which have been forged by volcanic activity are called igneous ("fiery.") Magma that has seeped up into cracks, and slowly cooled, forms intrusive rocks such as the very hard granites. Magma that has erupted as lava, and then quickly cooled, is called extrusive.

CAPPADOCIA, TURKEY

About eight million years ago, this region was deluged with volcanic ash, cinders, and basalt. Over the ages, the rock formed by these minerals was eroded into bizarre pointed columns.

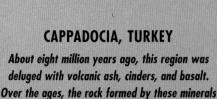

THE GIANT'S CAUSEWAY, NORTHERN IRELAND

It used to be said that the legendary Irish hero Finn Macool built this rocky headland as a road to Scotland. In fact, it is a formation of 40,000 or so symmetrical columns of basalt. They were created by fissure eruptions about 50 million years ago.

LE PUY, FRANCE

This chapel, in southern central France, is built on top of an eroded plug of lava. It is a reminder that many peaceful areas of the world have a violent volcanic history.

RISING ROCKS

Examples of extrusive rock include glassy black obsidian, slabs of basalt and andesite, named after the volcanoes of the Andes. Volcanic activity brings many precious minerals to the surface. Rich deposits of copper, silver and gold surround the Pacific "ring of fire." Diamonds, formed in the mantle, are carried to the surface with rising currents of magma.

Pumice is a rock formed from frothy lava that is full of gas. It contains so many bubble holes that it is light enough to float on water.

Diamond Hill is an extinct volcano crater in the heart of Honolulu. Inside the crater is a military cemetery for U.S. soldiers.

CRATER LAKE, OREGON

Crater Lake lies in the Cascade Range, in the western United States. It was formed about 6,600 years ago, when Mount Mazama collapsed, creating a vast caldera. This soon filled with rain and melting snows to form a beautiful blue lake. The little island in the middle is a new volcano in the making.

NGORONGORO CRATER

A giant crack in the Earth's crust runs down eastern Africa. Over millions of years, many volcanoes formed on either side of this Great Rift Valley. One was the mighty Ngorongoro, in what is now Tanzania. When this volcano eventually collapsed, it formed a caldera 12 miles (20 km) across, with a 2,297 ft (700-meter) high rim. The crater floor became a grassy haven for rhinoceroses, lions and zebra.

LIFE AFTER LAVA

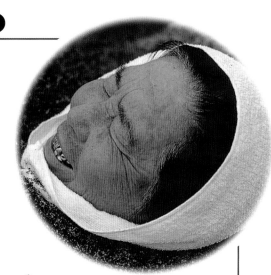

All around the world, there are extinct or inactive volcanoes, craters and calderas. Some of them look extraordinary, but others have become much harder to recognize. Years of erosion may have turned tall peaks into gentle mounds, covered in grass or forest. Craters may have filled with water to become deep lakes. In warm, tropical seas, colonies of tiny creatures called corals often form chalky structures on the submerged slopes of the volcano. If the inside of the mountain then collapses and sinks down to the ocean floor, these corals will remain in a large ring-shaped reef, forming an atoll.

Volcanic mud is said to have cleansing and healing properties, possibly because of the sulfur, also evident in the warm springs in health spas. This Japanese lady is buried up to her neck, having a volcanic mud "bath."

BEACHES OF BLACK SAND

Not all beaches are made up of white or yellow sand. Many tourist destinations have beaches which are black. These include the Greek island of Thíra (left), the Caribbean island of Martinique and the northern coast of Bali. All are volcanic danger zones. Their grains of sand have been worn down from lava flows which have plunged into the sea.

HOW AN ATOLL IS FORMED

FRINGING REEF

A volcano grows from the ocean bed. Corals grow around its slopes.

BARRIER REEF

The volcano collapses and begins to sink.

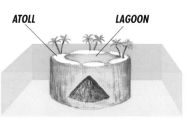

ATOLL   *LAGOON*

The volcano vanishes, leaving behind an atoll.

RINGED WITH CORAL

Coral atolls are rings of coral that are scattered across the South Pacific like a string of pearls. They have formed around submarine volcanoes, and teem with marine life.

VOLCANO SCIENCE

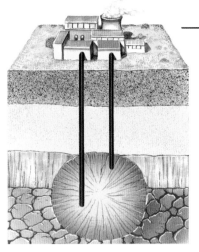

Volcanology is the scientific study of magma and volcanoes. Volcanologists try to find out how the Earth functions. In doing this, they may help to save lives and find new ways in which the destructive power of volcanic activity can be put to good use. Today, some volcanologists can study signals from satellites out in space, which use laser beams to measure plate movements. Others go down in mini-submarines to explore the oceanic crust. Volcanologists may also set off deliberate explosions and record the shock waves which return, in order to find out about the structure of the planet. They may even descend into the terrifying inferno of a volcano's crater.

GEOTHERMAL POWER

The heat given out by underground reserves of magma can be harnessed to provide energy on the surface. Heated water turns into steam, driving turbines that generate electricity.

ON THE BRINK

Volcanologists take samples from active volcanoes. They fill jars with gases and take samples of lava, which they can analyze back in the laboratory. They measure temperatures. A normal thermometer would melt, so they use metal probes called thermocouples, which measure conductivity.

SURVIVAL KIT

While working on the mountain, a volcanologist needs to wear a gas mask and protective clothing. Research is often very dangerous and some samples can only be collected by using special robotic machines.

SOME LIKE IT HOT

Tube worms cluster around a hot vent, in the Galapagos region of the Pacific. In recent years, scientists have used mini-submarines to explore spreading ridges. They have found that bacteria feed on the rich minerals given out, and that these provide food for tube worms and other strange sea creatures.

THE EARTH'S HEARTBEAT

Seismographs are instruments which are used to measure earthquakes and tremors. The information they provide helps scientists estimate the timing and strength of volcanic eruptions. The shockwaves increase dramatically just before a major disaster.

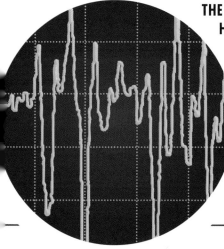

JAPAN, 1952
THE WRONG PLACE AT THE WRONG TIME

On September 17 1952, the crew of a fishing boat reported strange explosions beneath the sea. Their position was about 249 miles (400 km) south of Tokyo, on the Pacific rim.
A volcanic island grew up on the spot, but was promptly blown up in a new eruption. Japanese volcanologists hurried to the scene. The research vessel Sinyo-maru arrived and began to record the dramatic volcanic activity. Another research ship, the Kaiyo-maru, also sailed to the scene. It sailed right over a vent just as it blew. The crew of 22 plus 7 volcanologists were killed as the ship was blasted apart.

BURIED IN ASH

In Pompeii, the bodies of the victims were destroyed by the hot ash. However they left their shape pressed into the ash before it hardened. By filling these hollows with plaster or resin, archaeologists can recreate the bodies as they were at the time of death.

Plaster-casts show the tragic, huddled figures of Pompeii's victims. They are a moving memorial to all who have suffered from volcanic catastrophe through the ages.

THE FIRST FOOTPRINTS

These footprints were made about 3,600,000 years ago. They were made in soft volcanic ash, and as this turned into hard rock, the footprints were preserved. They were found at Laetoli, in Tanzania, Africa in 1976.

VOLCANOES OF THE PAST

This fine dolphin jar was discovered on Thíra.

One branch of volcano science has been of great use in studying history. When volcanoes bury the land in ash or lava, they often preserve people's bodies, buildings and streets, jewelry, pots, and pans and other evidence of everyday life. When such sites are excavated, it is like opening a time capsule. We find out how people lived long ago. The most famous example is the Italian town of Pompeii, buried by Vesuvius in 79 CE. The site was discovered in 1748. Archaelogists have discovered how Romans ate, shopped and did business, what their houses were like and even what plants were grown in their gardens.

• See page 60-61 for information on earthquakes of the past.

LONG-LOST PAINTINGS

These wall paintings, uncovered at Akrotíri, on Thíra, in Greece, show boys boxing. Other paintings show fashionable ladies, houses, and boats. When Thíra was destroyed by a volcano in about 1500 BCE, it was part of the fabulous Minoan civilization of nearby Crete.

When Vesuvius erupted in 79 CE, people were just sitting down to lunch. Food remains that have been discovered include loaves of bread, sausages, walnuts, olives, and figs.

VOLCANOES IN SPACE

THE MAN IN THE MOON

Earth's Moon has dark patterns on its surface, which look like a face. The astronomer Galileo Galilei (1564-1642) called them "seas." They are, in fact, plains of basaltic lava which oozed out from fissures and rifts about 2–4 billion years ago.

Where is the biggest known volcano? It can be found, not on Earth—but on Mars. And if we traveled to Venus, we would find volcanoes soaring to heights of 7 miles (11 km), hardened flows of lava and great slabs of basalt. On Io, a moon of Jupiter, ejecta are hurled from volcanoes at over 621 mph (1,000 km/h). Volcano science can help us discover how other planets and moons have formed around our sun. At some point in the future, humans may leave our Solar System and settle on other planets. If so, they will have to understand just how those planets were formed and the part played by volcanic gases in the development of their atmospheres.

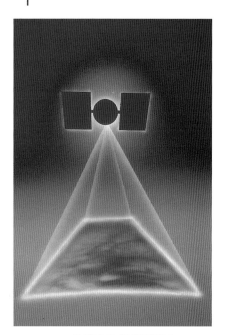

RADAR MAPPING

The Magellan space probe mapped the surface of the planet Venus in 1990-91. It used radar signals to penetrate the thick, poisonous yellow clouds which surround the planet. Venus may be named after the Roman goddess of love, but the surface of this planet is more like hell. It includes baking deserts and towering volcanoes, massive lava flows and hot spots where the rising mantle makes the planet's surface bulge outwards.

HOT VENUS

Sapas Mons is one of the volcanoes which tower over the plains of Venus. It is 248 miles (400 km) from side to side and 0.9 miles (1.5 km) high. This aerial view is based on a radar image beamed back to Earth from Magellan. At the summit are two eroded tables of rock. Around them is new, rough lava (shown here as bright yellow), giving way to older, smoother flows (dark brown, top left).

MARTIAN VOLCANOES

The volcanoes on Mars are probably extinct, but they are still impressive. This painting imagines the Martian volcanoes Arsia, Pavonis, and Ascraeus Mons. The biggest volcano known on any planet, Olympus Mons, rises in the distance.

Olympus Mons is a giant volcano, 15 miles (24 km) high—three times the height of Mount Everest, the highest peak on Earth—and a fantastic 373 miles (600 km) across.

JUPITER'S MOON

You can't get much more volcanic than Io. The gravity of Jupiter (the biggest planet in the Solar System), combined with that of Io's 15 sister moons, stretch and pull at its rocks, keeping them on the boil. There are major eruptions happening all the time, some of which may be as hot as 800°F (427°C). The moon's surface is covered in ejecta and splattered with sulfur, which colors it orange, yellow, red, and black. This picture was beamed back to Earth from the Galileo space probe in 1995.

The strange, volcanic world of Io was first glimpsed by the Voyager space probes in the 1970s. This picture, sent back from Voyager 1, shows a bluish gas being pumped out from volcanic vents. With little gravity on Io itself, the gases stream to great heights. They are probably made up of sulfur dioxide, while the dark area at the bottom is probably molten sulfur.

WHAT IS AN EARTHQUAKE?

ARISTOTLE

Aristotle (384-322 BCE), the great Greek philosopher and scientist, believed that the Earth had grown like a living thing to its present size. He also thought that our rocky planet was honeycombed with underground caves that sucked up the world's winds. When fires inside the Earth heated the winds beyond a certain point, they exploded. These explosions, Aristotle thought, caused earthquakes. It was thousands of years before scientists began to discover the real cause of earthquakes.

An earthquake is a shaking of the ground caused by movements beneath the Earth's surface. Strong earthquakes can collapse buildings, bridges, and other structures, causing great damage and loss of life. The Earth's surface is made up of an outer layer of rocks, called its crust. The crust is cracked into huge pieces that fit together like a giant jigsaw puzzle. These pieces, called plates, slowly move, and rub against each other, squeezing, and stretching the rocks and causing an enormous build-up of pressure. When the pressure becomes very great, underground rocks break and shift. This release of pressure sends out the shock waves that produce an earthquake and make the ground tremble at the surface. There are around 11 million earthquakes each year worldwide, of which about 34,000 are strong enough to be felt.

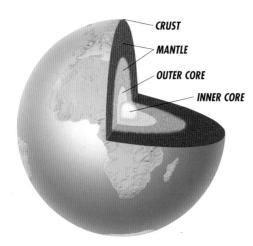

CRUST
MANTLE
OUTER CORE
INNER CORE

BENEATH THE SURFACE

Beneath the Earth's crust is a soft mantle, made up of hot, partially molten rock. The Earth's core is made up of iron and nickel, and is solid at the center. The crust can be up to 43 miles (70 km) thick beneath the world's biggest mountain ranges. Most earthquakes begin in the crust not far below ground, but sometimes they can occur up to 435 miles (700 km) beneath the Earth's surface.

ANDES MOUNTAINS

The Andes is the longest mountain range in the world, stretching down the whole of South America for 4,474 miles (7,200 km). The mountains were created by the collision of the Nazca Oceanic Plate with the South American Continental Plate. In 1970, an earthquake off the Peruvian coast caused a landslide on a high Andean peak, and more than 66,000 people were killed.

Curving strata are very clearly shown in this photograph
of a dry river valley in Namibia.

ROCK STRATA

**The rocks that make up the Earth's plates are themselves made
of layers, called strata.** As the plates move, the strata are pushed,
pulled, bent, and folded. The forces beneath the Earth are immense,
but movement at the surface is very slight and folding may take
thousands of years. If the strata are bent so much that they break, they
form a crack called a fault.

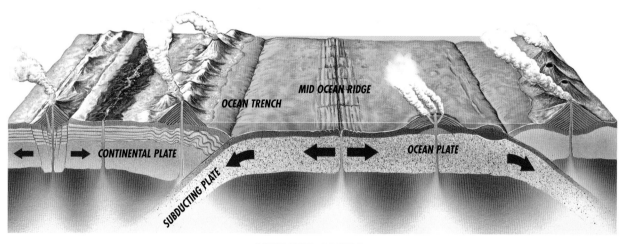

PLUNGING PLATES

**Some of the world's biggest earthquakes occur in regions where one of the crust's plates is forced beneath another plate as
the two collide in a process called subduction.** This is usually an oceanic plate, covered by sea, running into a thicker continental plate, covered by
land. The plunging ocean plate grinds against the upper plate, melting parts of both and creating volcanoes and earthquakes.

SAN ANDREAS FAULT

One of the world's most famous geological features, the San Andreas Fault, cuts along the Pacific coast of California, USA. This horizontal fault is 746 miles (1,200 km) long, forming part of the boundary between the Pacific and North American Plates. The two plates constantly slide past each other at a rate of about 2 inches (5 cm) a year. Many smaller fault lines criss-cross the region, some connecting up with the San Andreas. Every year, over 20,000 tremors are recorded in this area.

• See page 10–11 for more information on faults.

NORTHRIDGE, 1994

At 4.30 A.M. on the morning of January 17, 1994, an earthquake shook the town of Northridge, 19 miles (30 km) north of Los Angeles. The shaking, which lasted up to 20 seconds, knocked out 10 road bridges and closed three major highways. 60 people were killed and 25,000 were left homeless. Northridge lies on a small fault running from the San Andreas to the ocean.

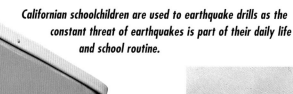

Californian schoolchildren are used to earthquake drills as the constant threat of earthquakes is part of their daily life and school routine.

SAN FRANCISCO, 1906

A huge earthquake shook San Francisco at 5.12 A.M. on the morning of April 18 1906. The city shook for up to a minute as the San Andreas Fault slipped up to 20 feet (6 meters) along 267 miles (430 km) of its length. About 28,000 buildings were destroyed, with entire streets collapsing. Out of a population of 400,000, at least 3,000 people were killed and 225,000 were left homeless.

The San Andreas Fault can be clearly seen from the air, like a deep scar across the landscape. Scientists think that the two ends of the San Andreas Fault are perhaps most dangerous: Cape Mendocino, north of San Francisco, and Imperial Valley, south of Los Angeles.

SAN ANDREAS FAULT

San Francisco

Los Angeles

NORTH AMERICA

This map shows how the San Andreas Fault runs the length of the Californian coast. The Pacific Ocean and the strip of land west of the Fault lie on the Pacific Plate, which is sliding northwestwards. The rest of the land is moving very slowly towards the south-east. Los Angeles, with a population of 14.5 million, is very close to the fault, and San Francisco sits practically on top of it.

SAN FRANCISCO, 1906
A SAN FRANCISCO JOURNALIST

The bureau at the back of the room came towards me. It was springing up and down and from side to side. It danced...in a zigzag course...it was almost funny. Now I turned on my sense of hearing. I heard the crash of falling buildings, the rumble of avalanches of bricks, the groans of tortured girders.

THE NEXT DAY

After darkness, thousands of the homeless were making their way with their blankets and scant provisions to Golden Gate Park and the beach to find shelter. Everybody is prepared to leave the city, for the belief is firm that San Francisco will be totally destroyed. Downtown everything is in ruins.

FRISCO ON FIRE

In 1906, most San Francisco buildings that withstood the shaking of the earthquake did not survive the fires. Many of these were caused by overturned stoves. Water pipes were burst by the earthquake on the outskirts of the city, leaving San Franciscans with little or no water to put the flames out. The fires raged on for three days, as survivors tried to find safe areas outside the city.

43

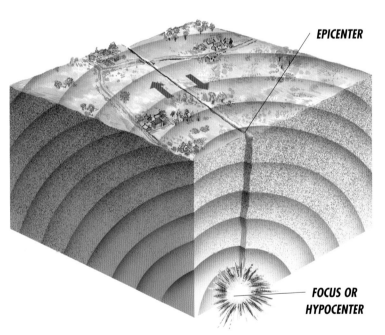

ALASKA, 1964

On March 27 1964, an earthquake hit the town of Anchorage, Alaska, starting a landslide and killing 131 people. Houses that had been built on loose rock and soil were carried a long way by the landslide, some as far as 1,968 feet (600 meters). The epicenter of the earthquake was discovered to be 81 miles (130 km) away from Anchorage, and the focus was 12 miles (20 km) beneath the surface. The quake also caused a tsunami which hit the coast of Alaska with waves more than 16 feet (5 meters) high and reached as far south as California.

EPICENTER

FOCUS OR HYPOCENTER

FOCUS AND EPICENTER

The focus of an earthquake is deep underground, at the exact point on a fault where the rocks first crack and move. The epicenter is the point on the surface of the Earth directly above the focus. Often the pattern of seismic waves is not as neat as it appears here: waves can be bent as they pass from one type of rock to another, and body waves can be reflected back down into the ground when they reach the surface.

SEISMIC WAVES

The exact underground spot where rocks jolt and cause an earthquake is called the focus, or hypocenter. This spot may be hundreds of miles under the ground or beneath the sea. The movement of the rocks causes vibrations, called seismic waves, to move out in every direction from the focus. The seismic waves move very fast, and we feel them when they reach the surface. They are at their strongest at the point on the Earth's surface directly above the focus. As the waves spread out from the focus, they get weaker. The general amount of damage caused by an earthquake's seismic waves depends to some extent on the kind of rocks that make up the vibrating surface. Solid granite and massive layers of sandstone, for example, shake much less than the sandy soil that is often found near rivers and coasts. When rocks begin to crack along a fault, they sometimes send out a gentle tremor or series of tremors before the main earthquake. These tremors are called foreshocks, and they provide a warning for people in the region to seek a safe place.

BODY WAVES

The vibrations that travel deep underground from the focus of an earthquake are called body waves. There are two kinds: primary or "P" waves, and secondary or "S" waves. P waves travel faster, at about 13,422 mph (21,600 km/h)—many times the speed of sound! They push and pull on the rocks, with an effect like a shunting train. S waves shake rocks up and down and from side to side in a snakelike movement.

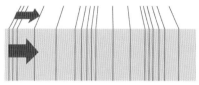

P WAVE

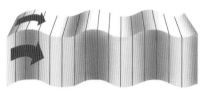

S WAVE

SURFACE WAVES

At the surface, there are also two kinds of seismic waves, named after the scientists who first described them. Rayleigh waves move up and down, while Love waves push the rocks from side to side as they travel forwards. Surface waves are slower than body waves, but they cause most damage to structures on the surface, partly because they take longer to pass through.

LONG-DISTANCE DAMAGE

One evening in 1989, at 5.04 P.M., the ground in San Francisco, USA, shook violently for 15 seconds. More than 28,000 houses were damaged, 63 people were killed, and nearly 4,000 were injured. Scientists later worked out that the epicenter of the earthquake was 75 miles (120 km) south of San Francisco, in the Santa Cruz mountains.

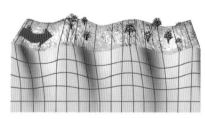

RAYLEIGH WAVE

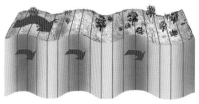

LOVE WAVE

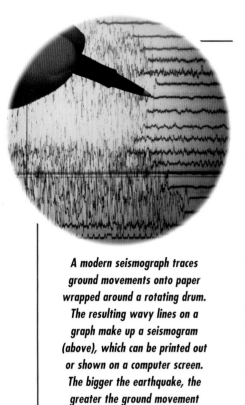

A modern seismograph traces ground movements onto paper wrapped around a rotating drum. The resulting wavy lines on a graph make up a seismogram (above), which can be printed out or shown on a computer screen. The bigger the earthquake, the greater the ground movement and the higher the peaks traced on a seismogram.

CHILE, 1960

To measure the largest earthquakes, seismologists also use the moment magnitude scale. This is based on readings for the size of the fault's rupture, the amount of movement at the surface, and the duration of the earthquake. The resulting figure is about the same as the Richter scale for earthquakes up to magnitude 7. The highest recorded moment magnitude was 9.5, for an earthquake on the coast of Chile in 1960, which also caused a volcano to erupt and killed 5,700 people. The Richter magnitude of this quake was 8.3.

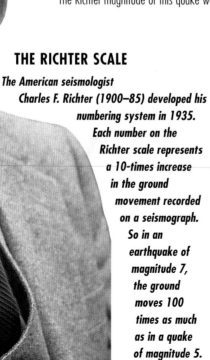

THE RICHTER SCALE

The American seismologist Charles F. Richter (1900–85) developed his numbering system in 1935. Each number on the Richter scale represents a 10-times increase in the ground movement recorded on a seismograph. So in an earthquake of magnitude 7, the ground moves 100 times as much as in a quake of magnitude 5.

MAGNITUDE	DESCRIPTION	AVERAGE PER YEAR
0–1.9	-	700,000
2–2.9	-	300,000
3–3.9	MINOR	40,000
4–4.9	LIGHT	6,200
5–5.9	MODERATE	800
6–6.9	STRONG	120
7–7.9	MAJOR	18
8–8.9	GREAT	1 IN 10–20 YEARS

MEASUREMENT

The scientists who specialize in studying earthquakes are called seismologists. They use measuring instruments called seismographs, or seismometers, to record the pattern of seismic waves and work out the strength and duration of each earthquake. Readings are taken at several different points so that the exact location of the quake's focus and epicenter can be pinpointed. The strength of a quake's movement, based on its effects and damage, is shown as a number on a scale. The first scale was invented by an Italian, Guiseppe Mercalli, in 1902. Today, the best-known classification of earthquakes is the Richter scale, which uses measurements from seismographs to describe and compare the strength and size of earthquakes.

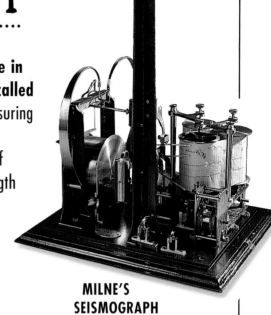

MILNE'S SEISMOGRAPH

British engineer and seismologist John Milne (1850–1913) became Professor of Geology at the University of Tokyo, and on his first day in Japan was greeted by an earthquake. Milne set to work devising his own seismograph, which recorded the movement of a pendulum, first on revolving smoked paper and later on photographic film. Milne collected the results of more than 8,000 earthquakes in Japan alone. He formed a Seismological Society in 1880, the first such organization anywhere in the world.

INTENSITY NEAR EPICENTER

RECORDED BUT NOT FELT

RECORDED BUT NOT FELT

FELT BY SOME

FELT BY MANY

SLIGHT DAMAGE

DAMAGING

DESTRUCTIVE

DEVASTATING

This instrument was invented around 130 CE by a Chinese astronomer and mathematician named Chang Heng (78-139 CE). Inside the pot was a pendulum, which would be made to swing by any Earth tremors. The swinging pendulum would knock a bronze ball from one of the dragon's mouths. The ball dropped into a toad's mouth. The position of this toad showed the direction from which the tremor was coming. It is said that in 138 CE the seismograph allowed Chang Heng to announce a major earthquake 373 miles (600 km) away, long before news of its damage arrived by messengers on horseback.

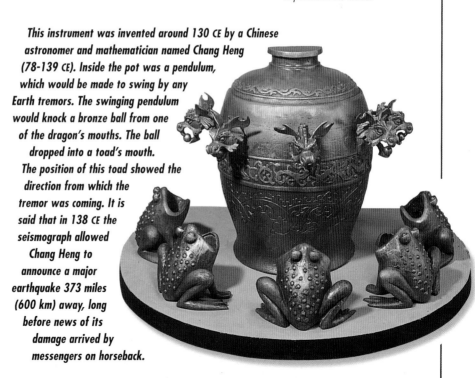

LISBON, 1755

MODERN LISBON

Lisbon was quickly rebuilt after the earthquake and today has a population of 1.8 million, and is a popular city with tourists. The oldest part of the city has steep, narrow streets, but in the newer districts, there are straight, wide streets and spacious squares. The docks stretch along the waterfront for 6 miles (10 km). In 1966 a long suspension bridge was built across the Tagus River.

On the morning of November 1, 1755, many of Lisbon's 275,000 citizens were in church, lighting candles for All Saints' Day. At 9.40 A.M., worshippers in the Portuguese city's central cathedral suddenly heard a terrible rumbling noise. The cathedral shook, and people ran out into the streets in time to see the ground heaving. Buildings throughout the city instantly collapsed and killed thousands of people. Many survivors ran to the harbor, but were then horrified to see huge waves approaching along the Tagus River from the Atlantic Ocean. The first of these smashed over the harbor at 11.00 A.M. There was even worse to come. Within a few hours, overturned stoves and lamps started fires that were whipped up by whirling winds. A huge fire swept through the city and burned all the wooden remains and many of the dead bodies. This terrible earthquake, with the resultant flooding and fires, killed around 60,000 people.

LISBON, 1755
FROM VOLTAIRE'S CANDIDE (1759)

They felt the earth tremble beneath them. The sea boiled up in the harbor and smashed the vessels lying at anchor. Whirlwinds of flame and ashes covered the streets and squares, houses collapsed, roofs were thrown into foundations and the foundations crumbled ... "This earthquake is nothing new," replied Pangloss. "The town of Lima in America felt the same shocks last year. Same causes, same effects; there is surely a vein of sulfur running underground from Lima to Lisbon."

CITY IN RUINS

About three-quarters of all Lisbon's buildings were destroyed. Records show that all of the city's 40 parish churches were damaged, and half were completely ruined. Fires burned throughout the city for days. Priceless paintings by masters such as Titian, Rubens and Correggio were burned to ashes. Most survivors left Lisbon, and many set up camp in the hills.

LISABONA

This engraving shows waves overwhelming ships in the harbor. Some buildings have been swept out to sea, and fires are raging. It is thought that one of the huge sea waves was as high as 39 feet (12 meters). Seismologists have estimated that the Lisbon earthquake might have been as strong as 8.7 on the Richter scale. They believe the epicenter was on the bed of the Atlantic Ocean, perhaps near the edge of the Eurasian and African Plates. It is also said that church bells had begun to peal thousands of miles away, waves appeared on the surface of Loch Ness in Scotland, and canal boats in Amsterdam were ripped from their moorings.

KANT

The German philosopher Immanuel Kant (1724–1804) reported that eight days before the earthquake, the ground near Cadiz, a Spanish port around the coast from Lisbon, was covered with worms that had suddenly crawled out of the soil. This was not the first report of strange behavior by animals before earthquakes and other disasters, and it was of great interest to scientists.

Engrav'd for the General Magazine of Arts & Sciences, Printed for W. Owen at Temple Bar.

A General View of the CITY of LISBON the Capital of the Kingdom of Portugal before the late dreadful Earthquake on Nov.r 1.st 1755.

This painting shows how the port of Lisbon looked before the great earthquake. Lisbon became the capital of Portugal in 1256 and quickly became one of Europe's leading cities. It was the chief port serving the vast Portuguese Empire.

TSUNAMIS

EASTER ISLAND

The great Chilean earthquake of 1960 caused three tsunamis that crossed the Pacific Ocean. On their way they hit the small volcanic Easter Island, which is almost 2,361 miles (3,800 km) from the South American coast. The tsunami knocked over some of the mysterious ancient stone statues for which the island is famous.

Seaquakes—earthquakes that occur beneath the ocean floor—can create **huge waves that sweep across the sea.** These waves are called tsunamis, from the Japanese for "harbor waves." They got their name because they are particularly destructive when they reach harbors, or any coastline. They are also called seismic sea waves, and sometimes tidal waves, but this is misleading because they have nothing to do with tides. Tsunamis are caused by the seismic waves sent out by seaquakes, which shake the ocean floor and then the water above. In the open ocean, a tsunami moves very fast, sometimes up to 621 mph (1,000 km/h). Out in the deep, the speeding wave may be just 12 inches (30 cm) high. But as the wave reaches shallower water near the coast, it slows down and at the same time builds up to its greatest height, which may be up to 98 feet (30 meters).

ASIAN TSUNAMI, 2004

One of the largest earthquakes ever recorded occurred in the Indian Ocean, off the coast of Sumatra. It triggered a series of giant waves that destroyed many communities bordering the Indian Ocean. The earthquake began at 00:59 GMT on December 26, 2004. 30 minutes later, the tsunami struck Sumatra. Thailand was next at 02:30 GMT, followed by Sri Lanka and India at 03:00 GMT. It wasn't until 07:00 GMT that the tsunami reached East Africa. It is estimated that over 200,000 people in 13 countries were killed in the disaster.

DAMAGE AT SEA

This boat was grounded by a tsunami that hit the island of Kodiak, off the coast of Alask USA. Tsunamis are very dangerous to shipping, especially if a vessel is close to the coast

This artist's impression shows what it is like when a tsunami hits the shores of Southeast Asia. The mountain in the background shows the great link between volcanoes, earthquakes, and tsunamis as any shaking of the sea bed can trigger giant waves. The buildings in the foreground will be swept away by the tremendous force of the water. A tsunami which hit Japan in 1771 was reported as reaching a height of 279 feet (85 meters).

NICARAGUA, 1992

On September 1, 1992, a seaquake measuring 7 on the Richter scale shook the Pacific Ocean floor, 62 miles (100 km) off the Nicaraguan coast in Central America. Many Nicaraguans did not even feel the ground tremble, but soon a 186 mile (300 km) stretch of coastline was hit by tsunamis as high as 33 feet (10 meters). The waves killed 170 people and left more than 13,000 homeless.

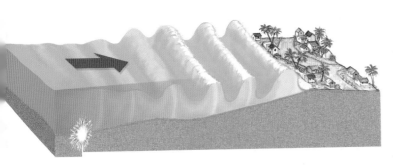

HOW IT FORMS

An earthquake shakes the sea bed, which in turn shakes the water above it. This sets off a tsunami, which builds up as it nears the shore. About three-quarters of damaging tsunamis occur in the Pacific, so Hawaii is the ideal location for the Pacific Tsunami Warning Center. Advance warnings give people time to evacuate coastal regions.

REFUGEE CAMP

When people's homes are destroyed by earthquakes or landslides, they need temporary shelter until they can start to rebuild their lives. Tents and other makeshift homes are also safer after major earthquakes, in case of aftershocks.

INDIA, 1993
BURIED FOR FIVE DAYS

Early on the morning of September 30, 1993, a large earthquake hit the Indian state of Maharashtra, killing more than 12,000 people. Seventeen villages were completely destroyed and a further 119 villages were badly damaged. In the village of Magrul, an 18-month-old baby named Priya was trapped beneath the rubble. Five days later, she still had not been found and her mother, who was in hospital with severe injuries, had almost given up hope. Then, as rescuers still went on digging, baby Priya was found, alive and well. The only worry for the rescuers was that the child would not accept a drink from anybody. They sent for her grandmother, and when she gave her water, the child drank. It was just that Priya would not accept anything from strangers. Today, the little girl says that she wants to be a doctor when she grows up.

PAKISTAN, 2005

On October 8, 2005 a devestating earthquake occurred in Kashmir, in Pakistan. The earthquake, which measured 7.6 on the Richter scale, was estimated to have killed at least 73,000 people. Kashmir is a mountainous region, and the terrain meant it was sometimes difficult to get aid to the people who desperately needed it. Landslides blocked many of the roads, and helicopters were the only way to reach many villagers. Rescuers dug for survivors buried under the landslides and rubble from buildings. They also brought food and tents, although it is believed many more people died from exposure and untreated injuries.

LOOKING FOR SURVIVORS

In 1970, the Peruvian town of Yungay completely disappeared beneath a landslide, and 66,000 people were killed. Landslides are such a common event in the Andes mountains that the International Union for Geological Sciences has started a programme using radar satellites to track them, so that scientists can learn more about landslides and mudflows and try to predict them in future.

These people are searching for survivors following a landslide in Peru in 1963, seven years before the terrible Mount Huascaran disaster.

LANDSLIDES & MUDFLOWS

Earthquakes often set off landslides, especially on steep mountains and coastal cliffs, which engulf everything in their paths. Where there is sandy soil or clay, the slightest vibration can bring down a whole slope. In 1920, an earthquake in central China started a large slide of loose soil that killed 200,000 people. Large rockfalls can be catastrophic, too. A magnitude 7.8 earthquake off the coast of Peru in 1970 started a landslide and avalanche of glacier ice on Mount Huascaran, the highest peak in the Peruvian Andes, and buried a whole town. Heavy rain can also cause rocks and soil loosened by earthquakes to flow downhill, and we call this a mudflow.

RESCUE SERVICES

In the Andes mountains and elsewhere one of the great problems facing the rescue services is how to reach people who need help quickly. Landslides and mudflows wreck roads and railway tracks. Helicopters are the most effective means of rescue. Even if they cannot land, they can winch people up from the ground, or lower or drop medical and food supplies.

MAN-MADE QUAKES

Earthquakes are caused by natural forces. But it is possible that humans can make them more likely by affecting the outer layer of the Earth's surface. Nuclear explosions used to be frequently carried out under desert regions, giving out huge energy and acting like earthquakes. Putting water into the ground can also cause tremors. This was discovered when waste water from a factory was pumped into boreholes under the ground near Denver, Colorado. It was stopped when scientists realized that earth tremors increased as more water was pumped in. Many dam projects have also been blamed for earthquakes, as the water in reservoirs weighs down on the ground below and seeps into cracks and faults.

• See page 120-121 for more information on dams.

CONTROLLING THE NILE

Before the Aswan High Dam was built to hold back the waters of the Nile, the temple of Ramses II at Abu Simbel in Egypt, built over 3,000 years ago, was cut into blocks and moved to higher ground to save it from flooding. The Aswan Dam was opened in 1971, creating Lake Nasser, a reservoir more than 311 miles (500 km) long. There were no records of any large earthquakes in the area, but in 1981, a magnitude 5.6 quake struck the lake. The epicenter was about 37 miles (60 km) upstream from the Dam, under the bed of the lake.

HOOVER DAM

The Hoover Dam holds back the waters of the Colorado River at the end of the Grand Canyon, on the Arizona–Nevada border. When the dam was completed in 1936, it created an enormous reservoir, called Lake Mead. As the reservoir filled up, tremors were felt in the region. When it was almost full, a magnitude 5 earthquake rattled the city of Las Vegas, 25 miles (40 km) away. Fortunately no damage was done to the dam, and the tremors died away. Today, the Hoover Dam supplies water and hydroelectric power over a wide area.

In 1997, villagers near a new reservoir in Lesotho, in southern Africa, fled when a crack 1 mile (1.5 km) long and 3 inches (7 cm) wide opened up. Since the Katse reservoir began to fill in 1995, people in the Lesotho highlands have felt many small tremors.

LAKE KARIBA

The Kariba Dam, across the Zambezi River on the Zambia/Zimbabwe border in southern Africa, made a lake eight times bigger than the lake created by the Hoover Dam. As Lake Kariba was filling up between 1958 and 1961, the region was shaken by more than 2,000 tremors. The biggest was magnitude 5.8. The tremors stopped once the reservoir was full.

Parts of the region around Lake Kariba have been made into a nature reserve.

WATER PRESSURE

We now know that underground water can cause pressure to build up and rocks to slip. At Rangely, Colorado, scientists tried a controlled experiment by pumping water at high pressure into existing deep oil wells. They measured the amount of water absorbed by the underground rocks and used seismographs to check for tremors. They found that the higher the water pressure, the more small tremors were recorded. It appeared that the water lubricated faults in the rocks, causing them to slip and shake the ground.

MEXICO CITY, 1985

The western coast of Mexico forms part of the "Ring of Fire" that surrounds the Pacific Ocean. Here the Cocos Plate beneath the ocean slides slowly under the lighter North American Plate, forming a deep underwater trench. At 7.18 A.M. on the morning of September 19, 1985, rocks slipped along a 124 mile (200km) fault in this region, moving a distance of 7 feet (2 meters) in two separate jerks, 26 seconds apart. The focus of the earthquake was 12 miles (20 km) below the surface, near the coast of the Mexican state of Michoacan. The quake released as much energy as a thousand Hiroshima bombs and measured 8.1 on the Richter scale. One minute later, the seismic waves reached Mexico City, 236 miles (380 km) away, rolling in at 15,000 mph (24,139 km/h). Within five minutes, more than 400 buildings in the city collapsed and a further 3,000 were badly damaged. Official figures listed 9,500 people dead, but the exact figure may never be known.

AZTEC CAPITAL

According to legend, the Aztecs were told to settle where they found a special sign—an eagle on a cactus grasping a snake. In about 1325 they found it, on a marshy island in Lake Texcoco, and built their capital—Tenochtitlan—there. The Aztec capital was destroyed by Spanish conquerors in 1521, and Mexico City was built in its place. When the earthquake struck in 1985, the vibrations in the old lake bed intensified, rattling the buildings in the city above.

MONITORING THE QUAKE

At the U.S. National Earthquake Information Center in Golden, Colorado, alarms were set off at 7.23 A.M., four minutes after Mexico City shook. Surface waves were monitored as arriving at the Center, about 1,553 miles (2,500 km) from the epicenter, another five minutes later. The Center issues reports on earthquakes throughout the world, and has located more than a quarter of a million quakes since it opened in 1973.

MEXICO CITY

A family who lived on the ground floor of a 14-floor apartment block believe they were saved by their pet parrot. The building collapsed on top of them and the parrot started screaming. Rescuers heard the screams and managed to reach the buried family eight hours later.

The Aztec capital of Tenochtitlan was a city of islands connected by canals. The waterways and gardens of Xochimilco, to the south of present-day Mexico City, are all that is left of the canals.

SEARCHING THE WRECKAGE

Rescue workers were able to pull many survivors from the wreckage of collapsed apartment buildings. More than 30,000 people were injured, and at least 100,000 were made homeless. Survivors can sometimes be trapped for days in collapsed buildings. Rescuers have the difficult task of locating survivors and then moving rubble safely. Specially-trained dogs and infrared or heat-sensitive equipment are used to help rescuers find people. In poorer regions of the world, where such equipment is not available, the rescue services have a much more difficult job.

CLEANING UP

In 1985, Mexico City had a total population of about 18 million. Most of the city's people were affected in some way by the earthquake. Many of the homeless were put up in tents until new accommodation could be found. At first they simply had to look after themselves. Disease can easily spread after any natural disaster, if there is a lack of clean water and healthy food. Some of the collapsed buildings were hospitals, and rescuers searching for survivors found a total of 58 newborn babies beneath the ruins. Some had been buried for up to seven days. It is thought they survived because their bodies behaved as though they were still in the womb.

HONSHU, JAPAN

TOKYO, 1923

These survivors searched among the rubble for their lost possessions. Two huge fires had broken out in the city from overturned stoves, setting the wooden houses alight. Fires caused most of the casualties. At the same time some areas around the city were lifted up by 7 feet (2 meters), and the floor of Tokyo Bay moved 10 feet (3 meters) northwards. The nearby city of Yokohama was also badly hit, and the *London Times* correspondent reported that Yokohama had been "wiped off the map."

Japan is situated where four of the Earth's plates meet—the Eurasian and North American Plates to the north, and the Philippine and Pacific Plates to the south. So it is not surprising that the islands have many volcanoes and suffer 1,000 earthquakes every year. Most of the earthquakes are quite mild, but in 1923, a magnitude 8.3 quake shook a huge area of Honshu, Japan's largest island, including Japan's capital city, Tokyo. Over half a million houses were reduced to rubble, and 143,000 people died, 100,000 in Tokyo alone. Then, in 1995, the very south of the island, about 273 miles (440 km) from Tokyo, was hit. The industrial port of Kobe suffered the worst damage with collapsing buildings and ruptured gas mains bursting into flames all over the city. Many of the city's newer buildings survived, however, because they had been built with earthquakes in mind.

KOBE, 1995

The quake that struck at 5.46 A.M. on the morning of 17 January 1995 measured 7.2 on the Richter scale. The city of Kobe shook for 20 seconds, and the concrete pillars holding up a 1,968 ft (600 m) section of the Hanshin Expressway linking Kobe with Osaka collapsed. The elevated expressway toppled and crashed. In all, 5,500 people were killed by the earthquake.

LIVING WITH QUAKES

Japanese children learn earthquake drills as a matter of course, including familiarizing themselves with special flameproof and waterproof headgear. In Tokyo, September 1 is known as Disaster Prevention Day. On the anniversary of the terrible Tokyo quake, remembrance services are held for victims.

NAMAZU

According to ancient Japanese legend, earthquakes are caused by the namazu, a giant catfish living in mud. In 1855 an earthquake struck Tokyo, which was then called Edo, and people believed that the namazu had been hurling itself around. It is said that before the 1923 quake catfish were seen jumping in ponds. In recent years, proper scientific studies have been made to see if catfish could be useful in predicting earthquakes, but without any great success.

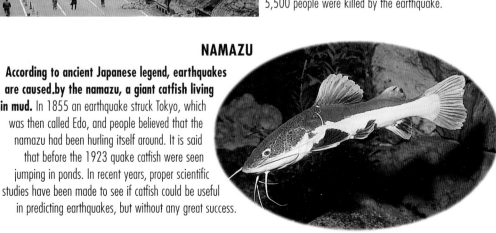

EVACUEES

The Kobe earthquake destroyed 100,000 houses, and a further 88,000 were badly damaged. More than 300,000 people were evacuated from their homes, and many lived in refugee camps for many weeks; 70,000 people were still living in shelters two months later. During this period there were thousands of small aftershocks, which made many believe that another major earthquake was on its way. Fortunately, this didn't happen.

The Kobe quake broke the city's water mains. About a million homes were without water for 10 days, so people had to queue for small supplies. Gas and electricity were also shut off, and 2 million homes were left without power.

TOKYO & KOBE

It was discovered that a 90-year-old woman rescued from her home after the Kobe earthquake had also been a victim of the Tokyo quake 72 years earlier. In 1923, she was working in an office in Yokohama, and hid under a desk to avoid being crushed as the building collapsed. She moved some years later when her husband was transferred by his company from Yokohama to Kobe.

POSEIDON

In Greek mythology, Poseidon was the god of earthquakes and later of the sea. He is sometimes known as the "earth-shaker." Poseidon was the brother of Zeus, and is usually portrayed as a supremely powerful god who was involved in many battles. The Greeks saw him as representing the violent forces of nature, and they sacrificed bulls in his honor.

EARTHQUAKES OF THE PAST

Earthquakes have been happening for millions of years. In ancient times, it was thought that all natural disasters were brought about by the gods. Earthquakes, along with lightning, floods, and droughts, were seen as signs that the gods were angry. Three of the Seven Wonders of the Ancient World—the Mausoleum, Colossus and Pharos—were shaken to the ground by quakes. The great palace at Knossos, built by the Minoans, had already suffered this fate around 1700 BCE. The citizens of the Roman cities of Pompeii and Herculaneum felt very strong tremors and in 63 CE, 16 years before Mount Vesuvius erupted and destroyed both. But at that time nothing was known about the links between volcanoes and earthquakes.

• See pages 14-15 for information on Mount Vesuvius.

THE FIRST MAUSOLEUM

Mausolus was ruler of Caria, part of the Persian Empire. He planned a huge tomb, the Mausoleum, for himself and his Queen, Artemisia, which was completed shortly after his death in 353 BCE. In the 13th century, the Mausoleum was knocked down by an earthquake. Hundreds of years later statues and sculptures, such as these which archeologists believe show the king and queen, were excavated at the site in modern-day Turkey.

The Pharos lighthouse was built in the 3rd century to guide ships safely into the harbor of Alexandria, in Egypt. This was probably the world's first lighthouse. At the top was a fire, and sheets of bronze reflected its light out to sea. In 1324, the Pharos was destroyed by an earthquake, and some years later the ruins were used to build a military fort.

KOURION, CYPRUS

On July 21, 365, a great earthquake struck the eastern Mediterranean region. Scientists believe that its epicenter was on the sea floor, about 31 miles (50 km) off the coast of Cyprus. The quake killed thousands on the island, and at the coastal town of Kourion archeologists have discovered skeletons, pots, vases, and many other artefacts, such as this mosaic, beneath the ruins.

TEMPLE OF ZEUS

The ancient Greeks worshipped Zeus, king of the gods, at Olympia. An enormous statue of Zeus, made of ivory, gold and precious stones, stood in its own temple and became one of the Wonders of the World. The statue was shipped to Constantinople in 462 CE, and about 100 years later, the whole region of Olympus was shaken by earthquakes. The temple and stadium were destroyed by landslides and floods, and were only excavated in recent times. Just a few columns (above) remain today.

Today, bronze deer stand on pillars at each side of the entrance of Mandraki Harbor, where Colossus once stood.

A FALLEN STATUE

Mandraki Harbor, on the Greek island of Rhodes, was believed to be protected by a giant bronze statue of Helios, the sun god. The statue, called the Colossus, had one foot on either side of the harbor, but in about 226 BCE, it was toppled by an earthquake and snapped off at the knees. The people of Rhodes were told by an oracle not to rebuild the statue, so they left it lying where it fell.

LASER TECHNOLOGY

In California, lasers are used to measure the tiniest ground movements with total accuracy. Laser beams are sent out from this station and aimed at reflectors on the other side of known fault lines. Sensitive instruments measure the time it takes beams to reach the reflector and back, so that any tiny change in distance caused by ground movement is detected. This is a very accurate system that can be constantly monitored.

HAICHENG

Early in 1975, seismologists noticed that water levels in wells around the city of Haicheng, in northeast China, were changing. Then small tremors started. Around a million people were evacuated from their homes in the region on the morning of February 4, and that evening a magnitude 7.5 quake devastated the region. Thousands of buildings collapsed and 1,328 people were killed. Without the warning, it would have been many thousands more.

地震
EARTHQUAKE
(shaking of the earth)

CHINA

GREAT WALL

HAICHENG

BEIJING

TANGSHAN

KOREA

重建
RECONSTRUCTION
(to build again)

YELLOW SEA

CHECKING GROUNDWATER

Scientists have found that the amounts of minerals and gases present in groundwater can change before an earthquake, as rocks move and the water is squeezed from one crack to another, so water levels are checked regularly.

TANGSHAN

Less than 18 months after the Haicheng quake, a much greater disaster struck the city of Tangshan, 249 miles (400 km) away. This time there was no forecast and no warning. The epicenter of a magnitude 7.9 earthquake was right in the city, with catastrophic results. The official death toll was 242,000, but it is possible that more than half a million people died.

PREDICTING EARTHQUAKES

Seismologists are constantly looking for new methods that will help them to forecast when and where major earthquakes will occur. Some scientists believe that strong earthquakes are less likely to happen in areas where weak quakes are common, because the small tremors relieve the stress that otherwise would lead to a major jolt. In high-risk areas in the USA and Japan, experiments are being conducted to detect the tiniest movements along fault lines. Scientists hope that this will help them predict a possible larger movement in the future, so that people can be evacuated from danger zones. They have also found that changes in the level and content of underground water can tell us a lot about the movement and possible cracking of rocks.

• See page 20-21 for information on predicting volcanoes.

CREEPMETERS

Creepmeters, which measure the creep, or movement, of a fault can be used to detect tiny changes.
Scientists believe that the more data they can acquire about small ground movements over many years, the easier it will become to recognize changes in the normal pattern. These changes may show that a big quake is on its way.

PARKFIELD, CALIFORNIA

Parkfield lies on the San Andreas Fault, almost exactly halfway between San Francisco and Los Angeles.
It is the most intensely monitored section of any earthquake zone in the world.
The arrows show the direction in which the fault is slowly sliding.

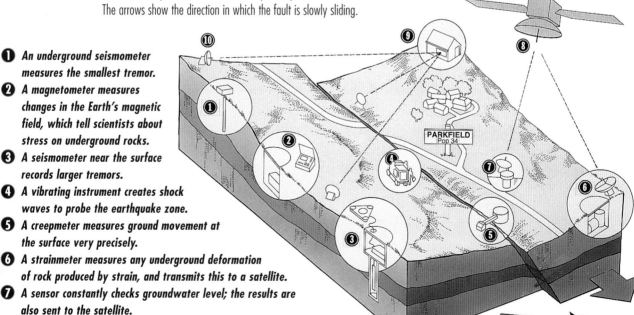

❶ *An underground seismometer measures the smallest tremor.*

❷ *A magnetometer measures changes in the Earth's magnetic field, which tell scientists about stress on underground rocks.*

❸ *A seismometer near the surface records larger tremors.*

❹ *A vibrating instrument creates shock waves to probe the earthquake zone.*

❺ *A creepmeter measures ground movement at the surface very precisely.*

❻ *A strainmeter measures any underground deformation of rock produced by strain, and transmits this to a satellite.*

❼ *A sensor constantly checks groundwater level; the results are also sent to the satellite.*

❽ *A space satellite receives data from Parkfield and beams the information to a main geological survey station.*

❾ *Lasers measure any ground movement across the fault by bouncing beams off reflectors* ❿*.*

LOOKING TO THE FUTURE

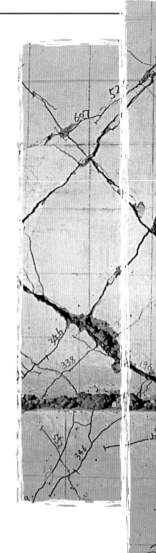

Scientists have tried to find ways of reducing the strength of earthquakes, for example by pumping water under ground to lubricate faults and allow rocks to slide past each other with less shock and **more warning.** So far these experiments have not been very successful, and we will probably never be able to stop earthquakes. However, we can try to learn much more about them, so that more precautions and warnings can be given, saving lives and also saving cities and towns from total destruction. Buildings can be constructed with earthquakes in mind, and modern technology can be used to forecast where and when disasters are likely to happen.

SHOCK ABSORBERS

Rubber and steel pads, called isolators, can be put under new or existing buildings to make them more earthquake-resistant —just like this exhibit in a California museum. The isolators act as shock absorbers, and the space around them lets the building shake without collapsing. Tall buildings must be able to sway without cracking, just as they do in high winds. To make them safer, walls are made of reinforced concrete and are strengthened with steel beams.

LEARNING MORE

The more we learn about earthquakes, the better we will be able to survive them. There are banks of seismographs and other equipment at the U.S. Geological Survey's laboratories in Menlo Park, California. Seismologists all over the world share information about past earthquakes and possible future ones. They also use computer programs to see what might happen in particular areas if an earthquake were to strike.

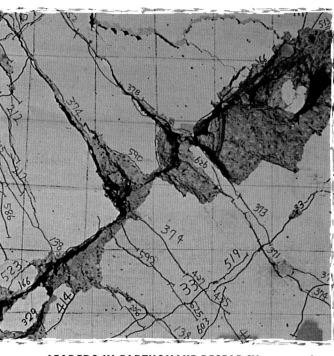

LEADERS IN EARTHQUAKE RESEARCH

The forces of nature reveal their secrets to a Japanese scientist, among the world leaders in seismological research.
The Building Research Institute in Tsukuba has the world's largest earthquake study facility. Architects and engineers use vibrating machines to test models of new buildings, producing the same effect as an earthquake and regulated to different magnitudes. The models are tested to destruction, to learn how much vibration they can withstand. Technicians map every crack after these simulated tremors.

SURVIVAL KIT

In earthquake zones, many homes and offices are equipped with survival kits. Their equipment and supplies can help people stay alive if they are trapped for a long time.

This pyramid-shaped 48-floor skyscraper is San Francisco's tallest building, at 853 feet (260 m) high. Its shape was specially designed to withstand earthquakes. It was completed in 1972 and is used as an office block.

WHAT IS A HURRICANE?

A hurricane is a large, very powerful storm with violent, whirling winds blowing at speeds of 75 mph (120 km/h) or more. Hurricanes, which meteorologists often call tropical cyclones, originate over warm oceans. They travel over the sea in the general direction of the wind, usually at about 12 mph (20 km/h), bringing with them heavy rain and stirring up high waves. When they reach land, hurricanes cause great damage and destruction. They blow down trees and houses, and the high sea waves and heavy rain often cause flooding along coastlines. Throughout history, hurricanes have been the cause of many terrible disasters. In recent times, scientists have learned a lot about how they form, but we are still powerless to stop them.

This photograph shows some of the damage caused to the city of Galveston, Texas, by Hurricane Alicia, in 1983. Twenty-one people were killed and it caused damage of $2 billion.

SHORELINE

A hurricane may measure more than 249 miles (400 km) across its spinning circle, and may last for many days before it eventually blows itself out. Ninety percent of hurricane victims are claimed when the storm first comes ashore. Beneath the center of the storm, the first tremendous winds and rain are followed by a period of calm as the eye of the hurricane passes overhead. Then the wind and rain hit again as the other half of the whirling storm passes over. As the hurricane moves across cooler land, it is no longer fed by warm rising air and starts to lose its power.

INSIDE A HURRICANE

When a hurricane forms, water vapor is picked up from the sea and makes thick walls of cloud. As the warm water vapor and air rise, they start to spin in an upward spiral. More warm, moist air rushes in underneath the rising air and the spinning air builds up to form a hurricane. The violent winds spin around a calm, cloud-free area of very low pressure, called the "eye" of the hurricane.

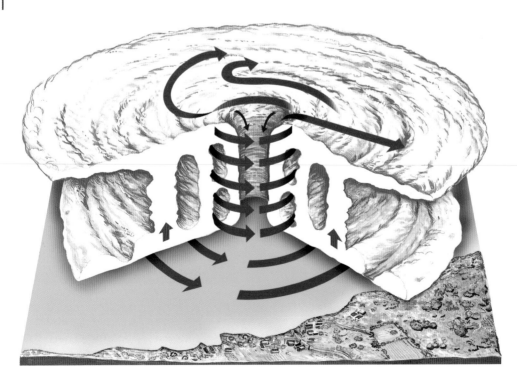

NAMING THE HURRICANE

Hurricanes are given names to identify them and to avoid confusion when there is more than one storm at the same time. The World Meteorological Organization chooses the names, which start from A each year and alternate between male and female names. In 1998, for example, the Atlantic hurricane names were Alex, Bonnie, Charley, Danielle, Earl, and so on. This infrared satellite photograph shows Hurricane Fran over the Caribbean in 1996. Fran's winds reached 118 mph (190 km/h) and the storm caused the deaths of 34 people.

This photograph clearly shows the calm eye in the middle of a hurricane, with thick white clouds whirling around it. At the top of the storm, dry, colder air from above is sucked down into the eye, which often measures about 19 miles (30 km) across.

WHERE IN THE WORLD?

Hurricanes start in bands just north and south of the Equator called the tropics: the Tropic of Cancer north of the Equator, and the Tropic of Capricorn to the south. These are the hottest parts of the Earth, and so their oceans have very warm water. Oceans with a temperature above 81°F (27°C) produce the warm, moist vapor needed for a hurricane to form. When severe tropical storms occur in the western Pacific Ocean, they are known as typhoons, and in the Indian Ocean they are called cyclones.

TROPIC OF CANCER

EQUATOR

TROPIC OF CAPRICORN

ATLANTIC HURRICANES

The southeast corner of the United States is used to hurricanes. In September 1998, Hurricane Georges caused great flooding to the low-lying islands of the Florida Keys. More than 150 homes were completely destroyed by the storm, which had already killed more than 500 people on several Caribbean islands.

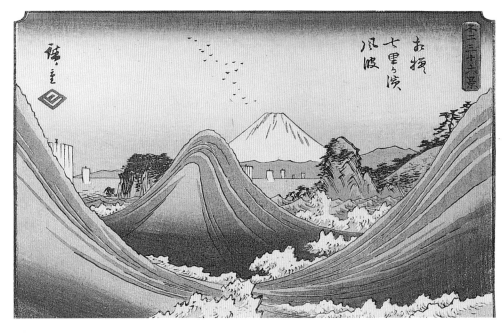

PACIFIC TYPHOONS

High waves and storms were a common theme for Japanese artists, many of whom had probably experienced Pacific typhoons. Ando Hiroshige (1797–1858), a famous Japanese painter and printmaker, created many landscapes and seascapes, including this picture of wind-blown waves.

STORM CLOUDS

Long, low storm clouds gather over the sea. Storms occur when masses of warm and cold air meet. The air masses do not mix easily together and cause winds, while clouds form along the edge, which is called a front. Not all tropical storms, however, turn into hurricanes.

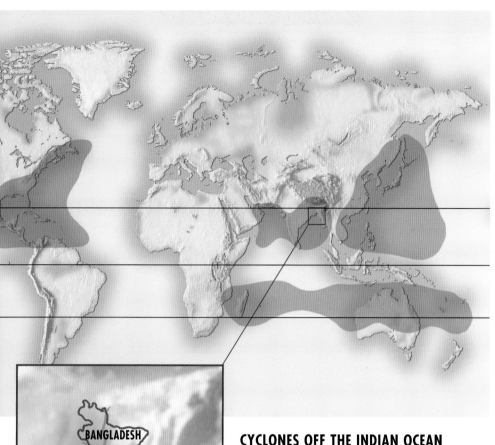

HURRICANE ZONES

The world's hurricane zones sit on the imaginary lines of the Tropics of Cancer and Capricorn and stretch across parts of the Atlantic, Pacific and Indian Oceans. Hurricanes usually travel westwards, pushed along by the trade winds. They then turn away from the Equator and pick up speed as they are affected by the Earth's spin. In the northern hemisphere, hurricanes always spin in an anticlockwise direction. Many hurricanes turn east when they reach cooler land or sea.

BANGLADESH

INDIA

Path of cyclones

CYCLONES OFF THE INDIAN OCEAN

This coastal region of Bangladesh lies directly in the path of many cyclones. The flat land of the Ganges delta is easily flooded, both by the sea and by the many channels of the river overflowing their banks. On November 12, 1970, a ferocious cyclone hit Bangladesh (which was then called East Pakistan). It caused a storm surge 49 feet (15 meters) high, and many of the islands of the delta were submerged. Up to 500,000 people were killed by the disastrous effects of the cyclone.

• See page 50-51 for more information on tsunamis.

STORM SURGE

Hurricanes whip up the sea beneath them and make huge waves. At the center of the storm, the low-pressure eye of the hurricane pulls up a dome of water up to 26 feet (8 m) high. As the whole swirling storm moves towards land, it pushes the large waves of a storm surge ahead of it. The surge eventually produces flooding on land, and in low-lying coastal areas these floods often cause more damage than the hurricane's winds.

ATLANTIC HURRICANES

The Atlantic hurricane season runs from June to November, but the most violent storms usually occur in August and September. This is when the ocean's waters are at their warmest. There are usually about six hurricanes every year, but sometimes there can be many more. In 1995, for example, 19 hurricanes were recorded. Most originate in the north Atlantic Ocean and then pass through the Caribbean Sea and the Gulf of Mexico, before turning towards mainland USA. In 1998, two devastating hurricanes struck one after the other. During September Hurricane Georges hit the Caribbean Islands and Florida. Then just four weeks later, Hurricane Mitch battered Central America.

AID RELIEF

Not only did people lose their homes to Hurricane Mitch, many also lost their livelihoods. Crops were destroyed, water became contaminated. Many of the world's richer countries and relief organizations gave money and supplies to Honduras and Nicaragua to help them survive the damage caused by Hurricane Mitch. Some of the devastated areas were very difficult to reach, and victims had to wait a long time before help reached them.

In 1992, Hurricane Andrew hit Louisiana. The worst devastation lay in a band 19 miles (30 km) wide, including the entire town of Homestead.

HURRICANE KATRINA

In August 2005 Hurricane Katrina struck the southern states of Louisiana, Mississippi, and Alabama. Despite a large scale evacuation programme, over 1200 people were killed by the storm and many more homes were destroyed. Much of the damage occurred in New Orleans in Louisiana. The storm caused the levees (embankments) protecting the city to fail, and there was wide spread flooding. Most of New Orleans lies below sea level, so the flood waters could not drain out of the city. Just a month later, Hurricane Rita also breeched the levees, causing further damage.

AFTER HURRICANE MITCH

Hurricane Mitch began as a Caribbean tropical storm on October 22, 1998. Five days later it had reached wind speeds of 186 mph (300 km/h) and hit land in Honduras. Over the next few days thousands of people were killed and more than 200,000 people lost their homes. Floods soon covered over half the country's land and three-quarters of farming land was destroyed. The Honduran capital was ruined. Thousands more people were killed in Nicaragua, Guatemala and El Salvador.

• See pages 76 and 104 for more information on Hurricane Mitch.

INTENSITY SCALE

Herbert Saffir, an American engineer, gave his name to the Saffir-Simpson scale of hurricane intensity. The scale ranges from 1 to 5, with category-5 hurricanes, such as Hurricane Mitch in 1998, causing catastrophic damage.

HURRICANE CATEGORY	WIND SPEED - KM/H (MPH)	DAMAGE
1	120-153 (75-95)	Minimal
2	154-177 (96-110)	Moderate
3	178-209 (111-130)	Extensive
4	210-249 (131-155)	Extreme
5	250+ (155+)	Catastrophic

HURAKAN

According to Mayan legend, Hurakan, the ancient god of winds and storms, dwelt in the mists above the great flood that covered the Earth. Hurakan kept repeating the word "earth" until the solid world rose above the seas. When the gods became angry with the early human beings, Hurakan punished them with storms. It is said that Spanish explorers named severe storms after the Mayan god, and the word "hurricane" comes from the Spanish word "huracán."

HONDURAS, 1998
SURVIVING MITCH

Laura Arriola lived in the village of Barra de Aguán, near the mouth of the Aguán river in Honduras. Her house was a distance from the sea and the river, but when Hurricane Mitch struck, the sea and river merged in a flood. Laura's house was swept away, and her husband and three children were drowned. But she managed to cling to some floating palm branches as she was carried out to sea, and then she made herself a small raft out of tree roots and driftwood. She found floating fruit and coconuts, and survived in this way for six days before being spotted by a ship and rescued. By then she was 75 miles (120 km) from her home.

The thousands of islands facing the Pacific Ocean to the east and the South China Sea to the west are particularly at risk. They experience typhoons from June to December, corresponding with the region's rainy season. In the Philippines, in 1984, two major typhoons sank 11 ships and caused more than 1,600 deaths.

Hurricanes and typhoons have been used as a theme in a variety of Hollywood disaster movies. This 1940s film, Typhoon, starred Dorothy Lamour and Robert Preston. Earlier, Lamour also starred in Hurricane, set in the South Pacific.

Causeway Bay Harbor in Hong Kong acts as a typhoon shelter for shipping. Whenever storms are predicted, it becomes a floating town, with junks, sampans and motor launches all moored for safety.

BIG WINDS OF THE PACIFIC

Every year on average, there are 11 tropical cyclones in the north-west Pacific Ocean. In this part of the world these storms are called typhoons, from the Chinese "tai fung," which means "big wind." These storms usually occur between the summer and autumn months of June and November and, travelling westwards, threaten the coasts of Japan and China. Many cross the Philippines and pass through the South China Sea. In the southern Pacific, below the Equator, there may be four cyclones threatening the Pacific islands, New Guinea and Australia, where they are sometimes known as "willy-willies," from an old Aboriginal word. These southern cyclones are most common later in the year, between December and March.

TYPHOEUS

In Greek mythology, Typhoeus or Typhon was son of Tartarus and Gaia. As shown in this ancient Greek sculpture, he was a monster with many heads, a man's body and a coiled snake's tail. The king of the gods, Zeus, fought a great battle with Typhoeus and finally buried him under Mount Etna. According to legend, he is the source of storm winds that cause devastation and shipwreck. The Greek word "tuphon," meaning whirlwind, comes from this legend, another possible source for the English word "typhoon."

KUBLAI KHAN

By 1279 Kublai Khan (1216–94), the grandson of Ghengis Khan, had conquered China and made it part of the great Mongol Empire. Two years later, he sent two large fleets of ships to invade the Japanese island of Kyushu, probably thinking this would be an easier task. But his ships were caught in a typhoon, and most of the 150,000 men were drowned or, if they were lucky enough to survive the typhoon, slaughtered by waiting Japanese troops.

THE PACIFIC OCEAN, 1902

FROM CONRAD'S *TYPHOON*

British novelist, Joseph Conrad (1857–1924) based his story on a voyage bound for the Indonesian island of Java, and on the character of his real-life captain, John MacWhirr.

Nobody—not even Captain MacWhirr, who alone on deck had caught sight of a white line of foam coming on at such a height that he couldn't believe his eyes —nobody was to know the steepness of the sea and the awful depth of the hollow the hurricane had scooped out behind the running wall of water. It raced to meet the ship, and, with a pause, as of girding the loins, the Nan-Shan lifted her bows and leaped...She dipped into the hollow straight down, as if going over the edge of the world. The engine-room toppled forward menacingly, like the inside of a tower nodding in an earthquake...At last she rose, staggering, as if she had to lift a mountain with her bows. 'Another one like this, and that's the last of her,' cried the chief.

THE INDIAN OCEAN

STUDYING STORMS

Captain Henry Piddington (1797–1858), a British sailor stationed in India, spent many years collecting information on ships caught in severe storms in the Indian Ocean. In his *Sailor's Hornbook for the Laws of Storms in All Parts of the World*, published in 1855, he called these storms cyclones, from the Greek word for the coil of a snake. Piddington also noted that a ship called the *Charles Heddles* whirled clockwise for nearly a week in a tropical storm off the coast of Mauritius.

I n the northern Indian Ocean, there can be up to six cyclones a year. Most of these cyclones happen in October, at the end of the monsoon season, when warm winds blow right across the ocean towards India, carrying a huge amount of water vapor. South of the Equator, cyclones happen later, around December time. On average there are about eight of these each year, half of which move southwards towards Madagascar and the coast of Africa.

FLOOD BARRIER

In Bangladesh, most flood barriers have to be built by hand. A major Flood Action Plan, started in 1992, is attempting to change the course of rivers and raise existing embankments. The country's capital city, Dhaka, is on a low-lying site on the Buriganga, one of the medium-sized rivers of the Ganges delta. The city, with a population of more than 5 million, is very prone to flooding.

RÉUNION

The volcanic island of Réunion, in the south-west Indian Ocean, sometimes suffers great rainfall from cyclones. In 1966, Cyclone Denise caused 72 inches (182.5 cm) of rain to fall in one day. Then in 1980, Cyclone Hyacinthe dropped 224 inches (567.8 cm) over a 10-day period. The economy of this beautiful island is based on sugar, which is grown on nearly three-quarters of the cultivated land. Flooding causes great damage both physically and economically.

WAITING FOR FOOD

Relief agencies regularly set up emergency centers in Bangladesh, where people wait desperately for food. The military are often brought in to help distribute the food as quickly and fairly as possible.

FLOODED OUT

Almost every year thousands of people are made homeless by the many floods in Bangladesh, which are caused, or made worse, by cyclones.

Most of the 120 million Bangladeshis are farmers struggling to grow rice, fruit, jute, and tea on small plots of land. Crops are often ruined by flooding as a result of cyclones, and then people are in desperate need of emergency food and shelter. A cyclone in 1991 affected up to 10 million Bangladeshis. In 1998, three-quarters of the country was flooded, claiming at least 500 lives and leaving 25 million people homeless.

This 19th-century picture shows the inhabitants of Mayotte, one of the Comoro Islands in the Indian Ocean, in a state of panic as a cyclone approaches.

BANGLADESH, 1970

LOCAL NEWSPAPER REPORTS ON THE DEVASTATION OF A CYCLONE

The small number of survivors are without food. I saw about 800 bodies lying on both sides of the dam badly damaged by the tidal wave. I saw at least 3,000 bodies littered along the road. Survivors wandered like mad people, crying out the names of their dead. There were 5,000 bodies in graves, 100 to 150 in each grave.

The tidal wave, as high as a two-storey building, has changed the map of the delta, sweeping away islands and making others. Whole communities have been destroyed and all their people and livestock killed.

BIGGEST STORMS

The most powerful storms are not always the most destructive. Reliable statistics of wind speeds, air-pressure readings, deaths, and amount of damage caused by hurricanes and other storms have only been available in recent times. They show that damage depends on when and where a storm strikes, and how much warning could be given. In September 1935, a category-5 hurricane hit the Florida Keys and killed 408 people. Yet a month later another hurricane, which records suggest was probably less powerful, caused about 2,000 deaths in Haiti, Honduras and Jamaica.

The National Hurricane Center in Coral Gables near Miami, Florida, keeps a close watch on hurricanes as they develop in the Atlantic and eastern Pacific. They issue "watches" and "warnings"—a watch advises part of the US coast that within 36 hours there is a 50 percent chance of a hurricane strike; a warning means that a particular part of the coast is in imminent danger and must take appropriate action.

FLORIDA, 1992
EYEWITNESS

I was on holiday with my family in Orlando, Florida, in August 1992. As Hurricane Andrew developed in the Atlantic and approached the Bahamas, local newspapers and TV reports became increasingly sure that it would hit Florida. By 23 August, everyone in the State was being warned to take action. They thought Andrew would strike Miami, 217 miles (350 km) south of Orlando, and told people to evacuate that area. Looking out of our Orlando apartment window, we saw that all the outside chairs, tables and sunshades had been sunk in the hotel swimming pool. Every movable item was put away or nailed down, and all available hotel rooms for miles around were taken by evacuees. The winds picked up strongly. Disney World attractions closed and there were tornado warnings on the 24-hour Weather Channel as Andrew moved across the State.

Neil Morris, the author

DEADLY MITCH

Hurricane Mitch set off a deadly chain of events in October 1998. Not only did it cause terrible flooding in Honduras, it also led to mudslides from the Casitas volcano in western Nicaragua. Mud washed down the mountain, carrying trees and killing at least 1,200 people. At the same time another nearby volcano, Cerro Negro, began spewing out lava and ash. This created a deadly combination of natural disasters.

HURRICANE CAMILLE

This category-5 hurricane hit the Mississippi coast in August 1969 and caused a storm surge over 23 feet (seven meters) high. The storm killed 256 people, including 12 people on the third floor of an apartment block who ignored warnings and were having a party to celebrate the coming of Camille. The tall building was flattened by the winds. Two days later, the spent hurricane dumped 30 inches (76 cm) of rain on central Virginia, causing mudslides and killing more people.

BOARDING UP

As Hurricane Andrew approached Florida in August 1992, the National Hurricane Center and other authorities advised and then ordered people to leave their homes and evacuate the area around Miami. More than a million people were involved, and very quickly every piece of plywood in every builders' yard had sold out, as people looked for materials to board up their doors and windows. Huge traffic jams built up on the roads leading from the coast. By the time Andrew hit land, at 4:52 on Monday, August 24, everyone was ready.

Even though Florida was prepared for Hurricane Andrew, still the unforeseen happened.

LABOR DAY

On Labor Day (September 2) in 1935, a category-5 hurricane hit Florida.

It had a low pressure of just 892 millibars, the lowest recorded for an Atlantic hurricane. The storm drowned many of the islands of the Florida Keys, and its devastating winds snapped wooden and metal structures, including trees and steel railings.

TYPHOON TIP

One of the most powerful typhoons ever measured developed in the western Pacific Ocean in October 1979. When it was at its biggest, Tip covered an area over 1,243 miles (2,000 km) across, and was powerful enough to blow this freighter ashore near Tokyo. Fortunately for Japan and the Philippines, Tip spent most of its time and energy over the ocean.

DESTROYING DARWIN

This twisted metal memorial stands as a reminder of that Christmas Day disaster.

In 1974, the residents of Darwin in the Northern Territory of Australia had a Christmas they will never forget. Early on December 20 a tropical storm formed in the Arafura Sea, an extension of the south-western Pacific Ocean. Three days later the tropical storm had become a roaring cyclone, with winds whirling at over 124 mph (200 km/h). Cyclone Tracy, as it had been named, rounded Bathurst Island and hit the northern Australian port of Darwin four hours earlier than forecast at 1:30 A.M. on December 25. The screeching winds blew everything away, making a roaring noise that survivors said sounded like a railway train coming out of a tunnel. Screaming residents ran into the dark streets, as their houses were torn from their foundations. Slowly the cyclone faded away, leaving the city of Darwin completely destroyed.

REBUILDING DARWIN

The Australian government set up a Reconstruction Commission immediately after Tracy struck. It was hoped to rebuild the capital of the Northern Territory within five years, something which was achieved in little more than three years. After the cyclone, there were only about 10,000 people left in the city. Now, Darwin is thriving once again and has a population of 81,000. Australian building regulations now state that houses in cyclone risk areas have to be specially protected against flying debris. In addition, their roofs have to be tied to the foundations. The authorities have taken steps to help people if such a cyclone should ever hit again, but they will always be at the mercy of natural forces.

DARWIN, 1974

BOB HEDDITCH, CAPTAIN OF A DARWIN FISHING BOAT

We put to sea on Christmas Eve at 19:30 hours and at midnight it hit us. The wind blew in our windows on the helm and tore off the back door. The waves crashed into the wheelhouse and I had to lie on the floor to steer. We had no steering by 02:00 hours, no lights and only the main engine to keep us heading into the gale. We lost both our anchors and I didn't have a clue where we were. We saw two boats send up distress signals, but there was nothing we could do. We limped back at 11:40 hours on the morning of Christmas Day. It was our engineer's first trip to sea. He disappeared when we docked. I think it was his last trip too!

TRAIL OF DESTRUCTION

About 10,000 homes, almost three-quarters of all the houses in Darwin, were destroyed by Cyclone Tracy. Sixty-five people were killed, the seriously injured numbered 145, and there were more than 500 minor injuries. Damage ran into hundreds of millions of Australian dollars. Tracy was a relatively small, but very severe cyclone. It measured 50 miles (80 km) across, with an eye of about 7 miles (12 km).

HOMELESS

As well as the winds, there was torrential rain: 10 inches (255 mm) fell in 12 hours overnight. About 25,000 people who had lost their homes had to be airlifted to other parts of the country, and by December 29. 10,000 people, including all the casualties and elderly people, had been evacuated.

CALM SEA

Today, Darwin is once again a calm, beautiful port. In 1974, as Cyclone Tracy was heading for the harbor, many ships tried to escape the approaching cyclone. Some were hurled onto rocks. Two navy ships sank in the harbor and one ran aground. Another ship was picked up and blown 656 feet (200 meters) inland. One observer said the harbour looked like a "junkyard."

WHAT IS A TORNADO?

On a stormy day in December 1879, just a year after it was opened, disaster struck the Tay railway bridge across the Firth of Tay in Scotland. Severe gales blew down a section of the bridge as a passenger train was crossing. It is said that two or three waterspouts were sighted close to the bridge just before the collapse. The train plunged into the river below, and all 75 people on board died. Boats searched for survivors, but none were found.

A tornado is a violent storm, much smaller than a hurricane, but with even stronger, whirling winds. The distinctive twisting whirlwind of a tornado hangs down from a dark thundercloud and touches the ground, like a spinning funnel. Some last for just a few seconds, while others go on for more than an hour. Most tornadoes move across the ground at speeds of 20 to 40 mph (35 to 65 km/h), and the damage they cause may be in a path over half a mile wide and 62 miles (100 km) long. The funnel of a small tornado may be just 10 feet (3 meters) wide, while a big tornado might be a hundred times wider.

DAMAGE SCALE

T. Theodore Fujita, a professor of geophysical sciences at the University of Chicago, gave his name to the Fujita scale of tornado wind speeds and damage. The scale runs from 0 to 5, with category F-5 tornadoes causing incredible damage.

TORNADO CATEGORY	WIND SPEED - MPH (KM/H)	DAMAGE
F-0	up to 116 (72)	Light
F-1	117-180 (72-112)	Moderate
F-2	181-253 (113-157)	Considerable
F-3	254-332 (158-206)	Severe
F-4	333-419 (207-260)	Devastating
F-5	420+ (261+)	Incredible

Amateur enthusiasts, or "storm chasers," sometimes have radar detectors in their cars to track and follow tornadoes. They keep a video camera with them at all times, so that they are ready to capture a promising storm on film. This dangerous hobby has provided scientists with useful pictures of many different kinds of tornadoes.

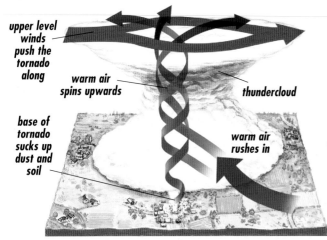

upper level winds push the tornado along

warm air spins upwards

thundercloud

base of tornado sucks up dust and soil

warm air rushes in

THE STRUCTURE OF A TORNADO

Like hurricanes, tornadoes form along fronts, where warm, moist air meets cool, dry air.
A thundercloud forms, the warm air rises, and as more warm air rushes in to replace it, the air starts to spin. The spinning air forms a tornado, which, in the northern hemisphere, usually whirls counterclockwise. The tornado, with its thundercloud, is pushed along by winds higher up in the atmosphere. Sometimes several small tornadoes can form together from one thundercloud. Dust and soil are sucked up into the funnel, which whirls around a calm area of low pressure.

WATERSPOUT

When tornadoes originate over water, the water and spray is sucked up into the clouds. These are called "waterspouts" and, although not usually as powerful as land tornadoes, they can cause great damage to shipping. The low pressure in the funnel makes the surface of the sea bulge upwards. Most waterspouts are between 20 to 197 feet (60 meters) in diameter, and sometimes they appear in pairs.

TORNADO ALLEY

Tornadoes happen all over the world, and are most common in North America, Europe, east Asia and Australia. In the United States, about 800 tornadoes are reported every year and around 70 people are killed. Waves of warm, moist air from the Gulf of Mexico often clash with cooler, dry winds from the northern states of Canada and the Rocky Mountains. This clash leads to many tornadoes forming along a wide stretch of country through the states of Texas, Oklahoma, Kansas and Nebraska, which has earned the region the nickname of "tornado alley." Most of the region's twisters occur in April, May and June, and they account for over a third of all US tornadoes. They usually occur during the afternoon or early evening, but there have been some night-time tornadoes. Florida is also often hit by tornadoes. It recently suffered when several deadly twisters hit Florida and Alabama in 1998.

TWISTER!

It is no good trying to simply outrun a tornado—it will almost certainly catch up with you. Anyone outside when a tornado approaches should try and move quickly away from the storm's path. If there is no time to escape the tornado's path, it is best to lie flat in the nearest ditch. Some houses in high-risk areas have an underground storm cellar for protection.

AREAS AFFECTED BY TORNADOES

THE ALLEY

An average of 125 tornadoes are reported in Texas every year, with over 50 in Oklahoma, 48 in Kansas and 38 in Nebraska. About 10 people are killed by twisters every year in Texas alone. This map shows how tornadoes are swept in by warm winds off the Gulf of Mexico.

TOTO

The National Severe Storms Laboratory is situated right in the middle of high-risk "tornado alley" in Oklahoma. Scientists there have developed a barrel of instruments that can be dropped in a tornado's path to measure its temperature, air pressure, wind speed and direction. They call this the Totable Tornado Observatory— TOTO for short, after the name of the dog in *The Wonderful Wizard of Oz*. TOTO weighs 397 lbs (180 kg) and is transported on the back of a special pickup lorry.

TEXAN TWISTER

Texas suffers more tornadoes than any other state in the USA. On May 11 1953, a single tornado hit Waco in central Texas, just 186 miles (300 km) from the coast of the Gulf of Mexico, killing 114 people. The worst US tragedy happened in 1925, when a group of tornadoes hit the states of Missouri, Illinois and Indiana, killing a total of 689 people.

DUST DEVIL

Sometimes when a tornado forms over a hot, dry region, it picks up a lot of flying dust and sand and is called a "dust devil." These dusty twisters seem to gather energy from the heat of the ground and can reach 984 feet (300 meters) up into the air. They are common in desert areas of the USA, Australia, India and Africa, including the Sahara Desert.

ACTION MOVIE

In the 1996 film *Twister*, storm chasers spent much of their time trying to get inside tornadoes to learn all about them. The film used amazing special effects to make the storms look convincing. On advertising posters for the film, tornadoes were called *"the dark side of nature."*

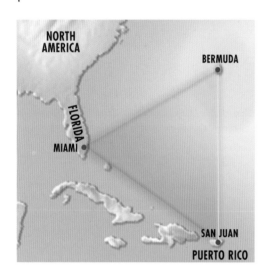

BERMUDA TRIANGLE

In the seas of the Atlantic Ocean between Bermuda, Florida and Puerto Rico, there is a mysterious area known as the Bermuda Triangle. Many ships and planes have disappeared here without trace. In 1945 a squadron of five US planes on a training mission vanished at the same time, and a search plane sent out to look for them also went missing. More than 50 ships are said to have disappeared in the region. One theory is that they were lost in storms, especially waterspouts, in that area.

In recent years there have been hundreds of cases of a phenomenon known as crop circles. A farmer suddenly discovers that some of the corn in his field has been flattened, usually in the form of a circle, making strange and interesting patterns. Some scientists have suggested that crop circles might have been caused by spiralling winds.

AMAZING WHIRLING WINDS

Hurricanes are easy to track, especially with today's scientific equipment, but tornadoes are often so unexpected and short-lived that we have surprisingly little information about them. Yet whirlwinds have existed throughout history; they have been mentioned in many accounts, including the Bible, and have formed part of many stories. One of the most famous whirlwinds formed the basis of *The Wonderful Wizard of Oz*. Whirling winds, tornadoes and waterspouts may also have been responsible for some of the world's great mysteries, which may never be solved.

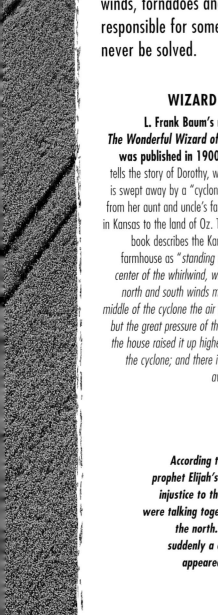

WIZARD OF OZ

L. Frank Baum's novel, *The Wonderful Wizard of Oz*, was published in 1900. It tells the story of Dorothy, who is swept away by a "cyclone" from her aunt and uncle's farm in Kansas to the land of Oz. The book describes the Kansas farmhouse as *"standing at the center of the whirlwind, where the north and south winds meet...In the middle of the cyclone the air is generally still, but the great pressure of the wind on every side of the house raised it up higher and higher, until it was at the very top of the cyclone; and there it remained and was carried miles and miles away as easily as you could carry a feather."*

IT'S RAINING CATS AND DOGS!

Over the years there have been reports of many strange storms, including some carrying animals. These reports were probably related to tornadoes. There have been showers of fish, frogs and lizards. In 1978 in Norfolk, UK a flock of geese were picked up by the wind, and in 1997 in Nottinghamshire, UK, pigs were seen flying through the air.

According to the Old Testament, at the end of the prophet Elijah's life, he handed on his fight against injustice to the prophet Elisha. The two prophets were talking together when a great wind came from the north. According to the Book of Kings, suddenly a chariot of fire and horses of fire appeared and separated the two of them, and Elijah went up to heaven in a whirlwind.

SAFETY PRECAUTIONS

TORNADO SHELTER

Underground storm cellars give the best protection against tornadoes, but any basement offers some shelter. If the building has no basement, it is best to lie flat under a table or bed on the ground floor, away from any windows.

In high-risk areas, the threat of hurricanes is always there. In some parts of the world, a television channel is devoted exclusively to forecasting the weather, but even with a warning, it is difficult to know what precautions to take. As protection from the severe winds, homes should simply be secured and people evacuated as quickly as possible, before the storm strikes. Barriers can be built along the coast and rivers to help keep back destructive storm surges. In Rhode Island, USA, a hurricane killed more than 250 people in 1938. Today, the Fox Point Hurricane Dam on the Providence River can be closed during hurricanes to protect the state capital, Providence, from flooding. Tornadoes are more difficult to predict and can arrive with little warning.

● *See page 116-117 for more information on flood barriers.*

These people are helping to build a high wall on the coast of Mindanao, the second largest island in the Philippines. After every disaster, the wall has to be repaired and built again. In wealthier parts of the world, higher, more permanent walls are built.

TEXAS, 1989
SURVIVING A FORCE-4 TORNADO

Gabriel Hernandez knew what tornadoes were like—he had experienced one in 1989. So he and his wife Maria Isabel dug a cellar beneath their home in Jarrell, Texas, in the heart of Tornado Alley. The cellar floor covered less than six square meters (65 square ft), but it saved the Hernandez family's lives. On May 27,1997 a Force-4 strong tornado slowly ripped through Jarrell. Twenty-seven people died, and the Hernandez's house was completely destroyed, but the parents and the three children survived in their cellar.

FLOOD BARRIERS

The best defence against storm surges and flooding are high sea walls. The 1,200 small coral islands of the Maldives, in the Indian Ocean, are especially at risk from flooding. Their highest point is just 10 feet (3 meters) above sea level, so the islanders have built special defenses. This one helps protect the harbor at Malé, the country's capital.

STILT HOUSES

In coastal areas all over the world, houses are built on stilts to protect them from floods caused by tropical storms. This group of stilt houses is on an island in the Moluccas, Indonesia, where Pacific typhoons sometimes strike.

Special road signs are needed to guide people to safety in a hurricane emergency without causing panic and confusion.

This storm cellar in the high-risk area of Arkansas was built above ground because of solid granite and limestone underneath the thin layer of soil. Reports state that it remained standing as fifteen residence blocks around it were destroyed.

WEATHER WATCH

There are thousands of weather stations around the world, constantly measuring air temperature, air pressure, and wind speed. More importantly for the forecasting of hurricanes and tornadoes, satellites watch and photograph the whole of our planet from positions high above the atmosphere. Their pictures quickly show where severe storms are developing. In addition, special planes and weather balloons observe and measure conditions in the upper part of the Earth's atmosphere. At the first signs of a tropical storm, computers are fed these details and also past information to enable scientists to predict the storm's course.

• See pages 102-103 for more information on predicting storms.

WILLIAM MCKINLEY

President William McKinley (1843-1901) said that he was more afraid of a hurricane than of the Spanish navy. During the Spanish-American War of 1898, President McKinley made the first effort to start a US hurricane service. Twenty-five years before, the first ever hurricane warning was issued in the United States, when members of the Signal Corps warned that a storm was approaching Connecticut.

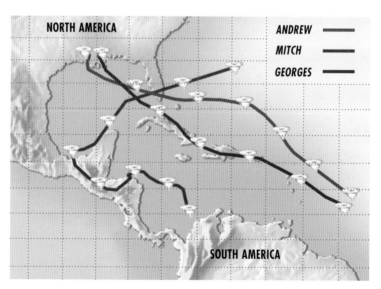

NORTH AMERICA

SOUTH AMERICA

ANDREW ·········
MITCH ——
GEORGES ——

Satellite tracking can help detect the areas at risk by a hurricane. This map shows the position of various Caribbean hurricanes at 24-hour periods.

FLYING INTO A STORM

Special weather planes are sent to areas where storms are building, to gain the latest information. They are fitted with a long probe in their nose and are used to measure air conditions at different levels of the atmosphere. On board is special radar equipment to give a clear picture of cloud patterns. A reconnaissance flight may last up to 12 hours, during which time the plane may fly into the center of the storm several times.

SATELLITE DETECTION

Meteorological satellites (or meteosats) beam picture signals to weather stations as they constantly orbit the Earth. These are checked by meteorologists to see if hurricanes are developing over the world's oceans. Four or five meteosats in the right positions can photograph the whole of the Earth's surface.

USING BAROMETERS

Weather forecasters use barometers to detect changes in air pressure. The barometer was invented by Evangelista Torricelli, an Italian physicist, in 1644 and measures the effect of air pressure on a metal chamber from which part of the air has been removed. Changes in air pressure make the chamber expand or contract, moving a needle on a dial. Modern barometers measure air pressure in millimeters or inches of mercury or in units called millibars. The atmospheric pressure at sea level averages 1,013 millibars, which equals 30 inches (760 mm) of mercury.

RECORDING PRESSURE

Scientists use a very accurate type of barometer called a barograph to record changes in atmospheric pressure. A barograph includes a pen that records the air pressure on a paper chart mounted on a rotating drum. Hurricanes and other storms build around areas of very low pressure, so barometers and barographs are very important instruments to weather forecasters.

FISHING

There is one possible benefit from severe storms. Fishermen have noticed that hurricanes stir up the depths of the sea. This disturbs the debris deep down, which is eaten by tiny creatures called plankton, which in turn encourage fish to feed. So without severe storms there would be fewer fish to catch. These fishermen are fishing off the coast of Venezuela.

BEAUFORT SCALE

The Beaufort scale of wind speeds was introduced in 1806 by Admiral Sir Francis Beaufort (1774–1857) of the British navy. Sir Francis surveyed and charted many of the world's seas, and he used the scale to describe wind effects on a fully rigged man-of-war sailing vessel. *Hurricanes are at the very top of the Beaufort scale of wind speeds.*

Force	Description	Wind speed-mph (km/h)	Force	Description	Wind speed-mph (km/h)
0	Calm	less than 1	6	Strong wind	25-30 (39-49)
1	Light air	0.6-3 (1-5)	7	Near gale	31-38 (50-61)
2	Light breeze	4-7 (6-11)	8	Gale	39-46 (62-74)
3	Gentle breeze	8-12 (12-19)	9	Severe gale	47-55 (75-88)
4	Moderate wind	13-17 (20-28)	10	Storm	56-63 (89-102)
5	Fresh wind	18-24 (29-38)	11	Severe storm	64-73 (103-118)
			12	Hurricane	74+ (119+)

FORCE 1

THE WORLD'S WEATHER

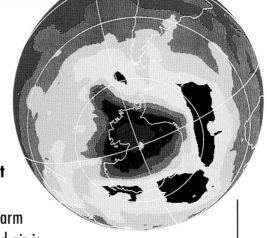

Extreme weather features such as hurricanes and tornadoes are just part of Earth's overall climate. When the sun's rays reach the Earth, they warm the air; warm air is light and rises, while cold air is heavier and sinks. The movement of warm and cold air causes winds, which in turn sometimes cause storms. In the past century, the Earth's temperature gradually rose — 1995 was reported as being the hottest year on record. This global warming is being partly caused by "greenhouse gases" in the atmosphere, which come mainly from some of the fuels we burn. This, along with other changes, could lead to higher global temperatures which, in turn, could result in coastal flooding, extreme winds and storms and other major climatic changes.

• *See page 104-105 for more information on global warming.*

OZONE HOLE

Since the 1970s, satellite pictures have shown scientists that a gap appears each year in the atmosphere's protective layer of ozone. The first hole was seen over Antarctica, as shown in red on this satellite picture, and the second over the Arctic. The ozone has been attacked by chlorofluorocarbons (CFCs), gases that are used in aerosol sprays, refrigerators and in making plastics for fast-food packages. Changes such as this might have a great effect on the world's weather.

GLOBAL WINDS

There is a pattern to the world's winds. Their general direction is affected by the spinning of the Earth, which bends the flow of air towards the Equator westwards. These tropical trade winds blow in the regions where hurricanes form. As warm air rises at the Equator, it is replaced by cooler air from the cold polar regions. This maintains the balance of temperatures around the world.

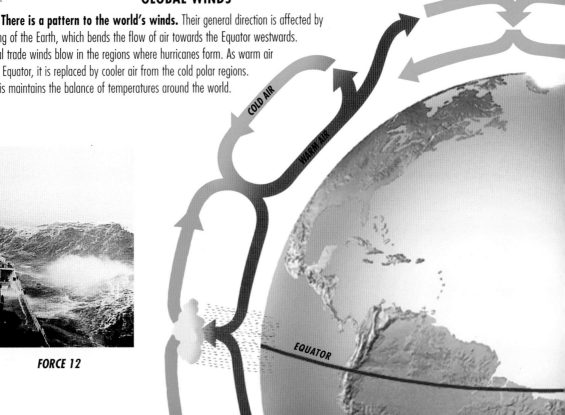

COLD AIR

WARM AIR

EQUATOR

RCE 6

FORCE 12

EL NIÑO

This damage was caused in 1997 by Hurricane Pauline, which hit the shanty towns of Acapulco, in Mexico, and was thought to be caused by the El Niño effect.

This oceanic and atmospheric phenomenon occurs when the warm waters of the Pacific Ocean flow eastwards towards the top part of South America, resulting in increased sea temperatures and climatic changes of varying severity. It is believed that El Niño is related to changes in air movements over the Pacific, which reverse the normal direction of the trade winds. El Niño is Spanish for "the child"; the name refers to the baby Jesus Christ because the effect usually begins around Christmas time. It occurs about every three to seven years and can affect the world's climate for more than a year on each occasion. El Niño causes increased rainfall, hurricanes and tornadoes in North and South America, and, at the other extreme, drought in Australia and Indonesia.

• See page 104-105 for more information on extreme weather.

WARM CURRENTS

This computer-enhanced satellite image shows the warm currents of El Niño, colored red, in the eastern Pacific Ocean off Central and South America. These currents warm the normally cool waters off the coast of Ecuador and Peru and bring torrential rain and flooding to the west coast of North and South America.

INCREASED STORMS

In the powerful El Niño of 1982/83, there was also an unusually large number of storms in California, but the 1997/98 effect is thought to have been one of the most intense. It caused a much greater number of tornadoes, freak storms and other disasters. There were violent outbreaks of twisters in California, and massive flooding in Peru.

This gold llama is an offering figure of the Incas. Around 1500 CE there was a mass sacrifice of 80 people by the Incas. Some scientists believe that this was a strong El Niño year, and that the sacrifices were carried out to try to appease angry storm gods.

SEARCHING FOR FISH

Pacific fish and the fishing industry suffer during El Niño years, especially off the coast of Peru.
Peruvian fishermen have to sail much further from home to find a catch because small fish, such as anchovies, die or move away from warm waters in search of food. Warm water at the surface of the ocean blocks the deeper cold water, which is where many nutrients are found. Many larger fish, such as tuna, follow their main food supply. This has a big effect on the country, since Peru is traditionally one of the biggest fishing nations in the world, catching more than 11 million tons of fish per year.

WEIRD WEATHER

This small plane was hit by a tornado while it was on the ground in Florida.
Meteorologists studying violent and freak storms are trying to work out how much El Niño affects the weather inland. Some believe that it has far more widespread effects than was previously thought. They have also discovered a similar effect that occurs in the Atlantic Ocean, and is known as the North Atlantic Oscillation, or NAO.

BUILDING A FUTURE

Amid the loss and destruction brought about by violent storms, there can still be a feeling of hope among the survivors. Communities are brought closer together by the wish to rebuild their homes and their lives. As a survivor of Hurricane Andrew said, *"We're alive and well. The rest is just stuff that can be replaced."*

Research organizations all over the world collect data from satellites and weather stations. They use powerful computers to process the data and develop programmes to predict future storms, and find out what might happen.

LOOKING TO THE FUTURE

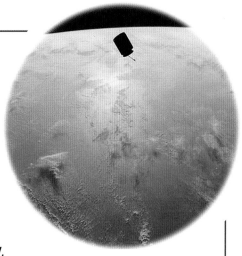

We will probably never be able to stop hurricanes and tornadoes, but perhaps we can learn to live with severe storms and their effects. Unfortunately, in many of the world's poorer countries—where a large number of these natural disasters occur—there are not the resources to cope with the phenomenal trail of devastation that results. Scientists and meteorologists are making studies all the time so that we can all improve our knowledge of these violent storms and what causes them. This will enable more accurate forecasts to be made, and provide useful information to enable more shelters and better defenses to be built, especially in the world's biggest danger zones.

STUDYING EL NIÑO

There is a special programme to watch and measure the effects of El Niño and other weather phenomena. The TOPEX/Poseidon satellite monitors ocean circulations all over the globe, so that meteorologists can improve their predictions. Every 10 days the special satellite measures sea levels to an accuracy of within 5 inches (13 cm).

LOCAL STUDIES

Information from small weather stations all over the world will continue to be of great importance. They add to the data being produced by large centers and transmitted from space satellites, and they are particularly useful in forecasting local storms.

HELPING POOR REGIONS

In countries such as Bangladesh, aid workers are needed to help local people overcome the effects of disasters such as flooding caused by hurricanes and tornadoes. The world's richer nations must also help those in need to plan for the future, so that they are better prepared.

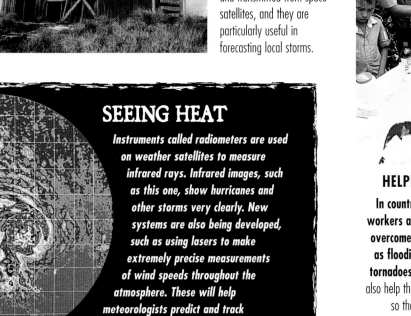

SEEING HEAT

Instruments called radiometers are used on weather satellites to measure infrared rays. Infrared images, such as this one, show hurricanes and other storms very clearly. New systems are also being developed, such as using lasers to make extremely precise measurements of wind speeds throughout the atmosphere. These will help meteorologists predict and track storms even more accurately.

THE UNCONTROLLABLE ELEMENTS

Before the construction of the Aswan Dam on the River Nile in Egypt, the river used to flood once every year, irrigating the soil. When the floods went down again, the land was left with a covering of natural fertilizer that helped crops to grow. For centuries, farmers along the Nile relied on its annual floods to raise their crops of barley, wheat, and millet.

Fires and floods often make headline news. When a fire rages out of control setting light to everything in its path, or a river bursts its banks sending swirling water through streets and buildings, the results can be disastrous. Although we have developed ways to protect ourselves, we cannot control the power of these natural forces. A fire may start as the result of a lightning strike, or from the heat of lava erupting out of a volcano. A flood is just one part of the great water cycle that distributes water across our planet. Both fires and floods can cause terrible devastation and loss of life, but they can also bring great benefits to the environment, wildlife, and to people.

LIVING WITH FLOODS

In some regions of the world, people have little choice but to live with regular flooding.

The country most severely affected by floods is Bangladesh. This is because about 80 percent of Bangladesh is a vast floodplain for three great rivers, the Ganges, the Brahmaputra (Jamuna) and the Meghna. The country is also often hit by cyclones (hurricanes) which can cause huge storm surges and coastal flooding.

FIRE CLEARANCE

From ancient times, fire has been used to help grow crops. In the tropical rain forests, people cut and burned small clearings in the trees where they planted their crops. When the soil was exhausted they moved on to a new patch, allowing the forest to grow back over the old clearing. This kind of agriculture is known as shifting cultivation, and it is still practised by some forest peoples.

VITAL FIRE

From the earliest times, fire has been important for survival. Fire provides warmth, and it can be used to cook food. In many places, fire was an important part of religious ceremonies, and some people worshipped fire — the bringer of both heat and light.

LISBON, 1755

When a huge earthquake hit the city of Lisbon, Portugal, in 1755, it resulted in both flood and fire. Minutes after the quake struck, three huge waves swept up the River Tagus and engulfed much of the lower half of the city. Meanwhile, numerous candles and cooking fires set the wreckage of the buildings alight.
• *See pages 48-49 for more information on the Lisbon earthquake.*

A spectacular storm sends streaks of lightning to the ground in Tucson, Arizona. Not all lightning strikes start fires, but lightning fires are much more common in some parts of the world than others. Scientists have calculated that lightning starts about 65 percent of all wildfires in western USA, but only about eight percent of bushfires in Australia.

BLACK DRAGON FIRE

In the northeast of China lies the Hinggan forest. Through the middle of the forest runs the Black Dragon (Amur) River. For centuries, lightning fires have burned through the forest, leaving scars which are eventually covered over with new growth. But the fire that broke out on May 6, 1987 started from lighted cigarettes igniting some spilt petrol. It was quickly spread by strong winds, and despite attempts to control it, the fire burned until May 12. It destroyed about 20 percent of China's forest reserves, killed over 200 people, and left over 50,000 homeless.

FIRES: WHY DO THEY HAPPEN?

The two main causes of fire in the environment are **lightning and human activity.** On average, lightning strikes the ground 100,000 times every day—although not all these strikes start a fire. However, it is people who cause the majority of countryside fires, mostly through carelessness. Throwing away a lighted match or glowing cigarette end can have catastrophic consequences—but a surprising number of fires are started deliberately. In some places, a fire can start without any immediately obvious cause. This is called spontaneous combustion, and it can happen when there is a large build up of dead and rotting vegetation, which produces heat.

A campfire should be set on rock or bare ground to prevent vegetation around the fire from catching light. In some wilderness areas fires may not be permitted because of the high risk of forest fires.

FIRE TRIANGLE

What do you need to make fire? The three essential ingredients for a fire are heat, fuel and oxygen. These make up the "fire triangle." For a fire to start, the fuel must heat to a certain temperature (called ignition point) and there must be oxygen for the fuel to react with. If one part of the fire triangle is missing, a fire cannot burn. For example, if you throw a fire blanket over a small fire, the fire should go out because it is starved of oxygen.

STARTING A FIRE

Most fires in the countryside are started by carelessness.
Many people do not realize the danger of throwing away a lighted cigarette or match into dry undergrowth, or of not controlling and putting out a campfire properly. Another cause of fire is the sparks from machinery—from wheels of trains as they run along metal tracks, or from equipment used by lumbering companies. Meanwhile, it is estimated that about 25 percent of all forest fires in the USA are started on purpose.

SEASONAL FLOODS

Flooding doesn't stop life carrying on as normal in Varanasi, northeast India.
Varanasi stands on the River Ganges, and the city streets are often filled with water during the summer monsoon season. There are two monsoon seasons in southern Asia. The winter monsoon brings hot, dry weather; during the summer monsoon there are heavy rains, which swell rivers and cause regular flooding.

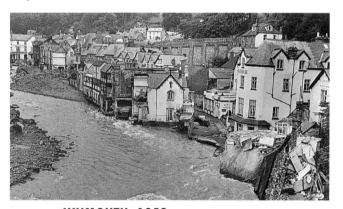

LYNMOUTH, 1952

The town of Lynmouth, in Devon, England stands at the mouth of two rivers, the West and East Lyn which tumble 1,476 feet (450 meters) down picturesque gorges before reaching the sea.
The rainfall on August 15, 1952 was one of the heaviest ever recorded in Great Britain and both rivers were soon swollen with water. During the night, a wall of water over 30 feet (9 meters) high swept through the town, demolishing houses in its path, sweeping cars far out to sea and depositing huge boulders on the beach. This flash flood killed at least 34 people.

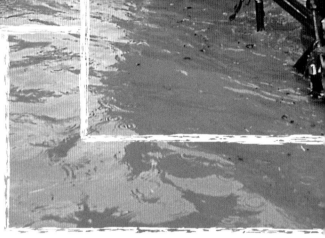

TSUNAMIS

This artwork shows a tsunami about to swamp a coastal village, as a result of an earthquake under the ocean bed. In the middle of the ocean the tsunami is fast-moving but often barely detectable, with a crest only three feet (one meter) high. But as it reaches shallower water the tsunami slows down, and the water in the wave starts to pile up. The biggest tsunamis can reach up to a terrifying 82 feet (25 meters in height.
• See pages 50-51 for more information on tsunamis.

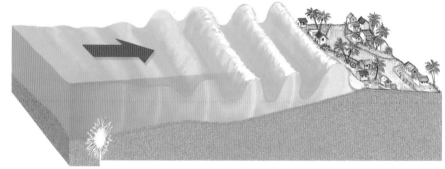

FLOODS: WHY DO THEY HAPPEN?

What is a flood? Floods happen when water rises beyond its normal level and overflows on to land that isn't usually submerged. The water can come from streams and rivers or, along coastlines, from the sea. There are many different reasons why rivers burst their banks. The most common cause of flooding is heavy rain, as well as melting ice and snow from mountainous regions. In coastal areas, massive storms such as hurricanes can whip up huge waves, pushing vast amounts of water inland. Floods can also result from landslides, dam failures, earthquakes and volcanic activity. Often it is a combination of several problems that leads to flooding. Flash floods are particularly dangerous. These violent floods happen suddenly and often without any warning.

A CATASTROPHIC WAVE

Dam failure, when a dam breaks and allows water to escape, has been the cause of some major floods. But during the catastrophe that overwhelmed an Alpine valley in 1963 the dam did not fail. The Vaiont Dam was built 846 feet (258 meters) high at the head of a valley in northeastern Italy. Above it stood the steep slopes of Mount Toc. On the night of October 9, after heavy rain, the unstable slopes of the mountain slid into the reservoir, sending a massive wave 325 feet (99 meters) over the top of the dam. In only 15 minutes, this giant wave swept through the valley below the dam, killing 2,600 people.

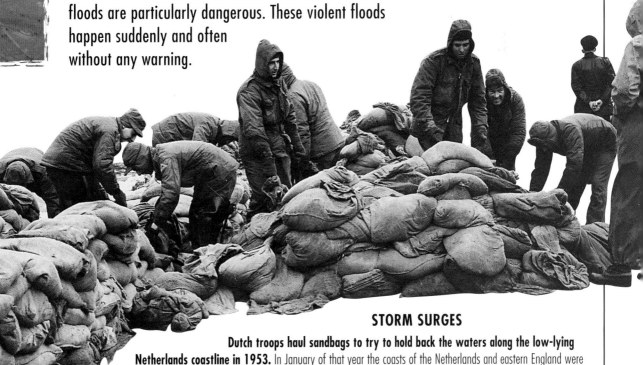

STORM SURGES

Dutch troops haul sandbags to try to hold back the waters along the low-lying Netherlands coastline in 1953. In January of that year the coasts of the Netherlands and eastern England were battered by storms. Towards the end of the month, the gales coincided with a very high tide and, during the night of January 31, the seas poured over the tops of the dykes protecting land and homes in the Netherlands. The storm surge flooded over 100,000 hectares of Dutch farmland with salt water, and drowned over 1,500 people.

SIGNS & WARNINGS

If lives are to be saved, it is vital to have good systems to warn people where and when fires and floods are likely to happen. Weather forecasting is the first priority. Today, meteorologists can accurately predict what the weather will do for a few days ahead. Fire researchers use this information together with their specialized knowledge to assess the likelihood of a fire. If a fire is already burning, they look at factors such as temperature, wind direction, and speed to try to work out how the fire will behave. Hydrologists (scientists who specialize in the behavior of water) also use weather information. However, predicting exactly where a flood might happen isn't easy. Heavy rain in one area may run away harmlessly, but in another area a cloudburst may cause a flash flood. Hydrologists use their knowledge about each particular area to assess the risk of flooding.

• *See pages 88-89 for more information on predicting hurricanes and tornadoes.*

HURRICANE ALERT

This satellite picture of Hurricane Andrew shows the distinctive whorl shape of hurricane clouds with the "eye" at the center. Big hurricanes bring torrential rain and strong winds. If they hit coastal areas they can cause huge waves and storm surges. Using satellite pictures, meteorologists track hurricanes and try to predict where they will go next. If a severe hurricane threatens to hit a populated area, whole regions are sometimes evacuated.

Water falls to the ground in the form of rain and snow

Trees and plants give off water vapor

Water vapor from oceans, lakes and rivers evaporates and cools to form clouds

Some water seeps into the ground. Eventually it flows down, back into the rivers and oceans

THE WATER CYCLE

All the water on Earth is involved in an endless cycle in which it moves from the surface of the Earth into the atmosphere and then back again. This constant movement is called the water (or hydrological) cycle. Water rises into the atmosphere, cools, condenses, and returns to the Earth's surface as rain or snow. Then the water either evaporates straight back into the atmosphere, or is carried by rivers to the sea, or goes deep underground. Some is locked as ice into icecaps and glaciers. It may take thousands of years, but eventually all of this water will evaporate back into the atmosphere, where it will once again condense and fall back to Earth... And so the cycle continues.

In the USA, a flood watch/flash flood watch is issued when a flood is possible. Flood warning/flash flood warnings are more serious and mean that floods are expected in your area and you should evacuate to higher ground immediately.

FLOOD WARNING

The United States of America has a very well-organized and up-to-date system of flood warning run by the National Weather Service of National Oceanic and Atmospheric Administration (NOAA). Information comes from the National Meteorological Center and is fed to 13 River Forecast Centers. Hydrologists at these centers prepare a flood forecast which is passed on to Weather Forecast Offices. If necessary, warning of a flood is issued to radio, television, newspapers, police, and other agencies. Many other countries operate similar systems.

A fire alert board in the USA warns of the fire danger in a particular area. The board shows that this region is on the second highest alert for fire. The risk of fire is assessed by collecting information from various sources about the weather (temperature, wind, and rainfall), and the amount of "fuel" lying on the ground in a particular area and how dry it is.

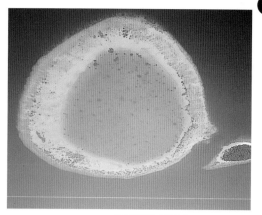

EXTREME WEATHER

1998 was the worst year on record for natural disasters. **Heatwaves caused drought in many parts of the world leading to massive forest fires in Southeast Asia and the Amazon.** In Florida, USA, thousands of people were evacuated from their homes because of forest fires. Meanwhile, torrential rain brought terrible flooding to Bangladesh and to China, where over 2,500 people drowned. Finally, Hurricane Mitch swept Honduras, killing more than 10,000 people. Scientists are predicting this pattern for years to come. Many think that one of the reasons for the increase in flood and fire disasters in the 20th century is climate change. As the world heats up, there is more energy to drive the water cycle and other climate systems resulting in more extreme temperatures, rainfall and winds.

• See pages 90-91 for more information on global warming.

RISING SEAS

Some scientists predict the sea level could rise enough to flood many coastal areas, and to leave some islands, such as the Maldive Islands, permanently underwater. Climate change could cause the vast ice sheets at the North and South Poles to melt, unlocking huge amounts of water into the seas and oceans.

MITCH WREAKS HAVOC

In late September 1998 a hurricane formed over the South Caribbean Sea. It was named Hurricane Mitch, and it was destined to be the most ferocious hurricane to hit the Caribbean since Hurricane Gilbert in 1988. At the end of October, Hurricane Mitch swept across Honduras in Central America, causing catastrophic flooding and mudslides. By November 2, over 10,000 people had died in Honduras.

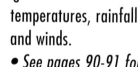

BEING PREPARED

The summer of 1993-4 was extremely hot and dry in Australia. There was no rain for weeks, and temperatures were regularly above average. All of this pointed to an extremely high fire risk and, in January 1994, several bushfires broke out. The fires swept through New South Wales and threatened the outskirts of Sydney. Yet, good organization and preparation meant that total disaster was averted and, amazingly, only four people lost their lives.

VOLCANIC POLLUTION

The gases causing global warming are known as "greenhouse gases" and come from air pollution from industry, vehicle exhausts and from nature itself. Erupting volcanoes spew out huge clouds of ash and gases that can affect weather worldwide. The haze that floated in the air after a huge eruption in Iceland in 1783 reduced the amount of sunlight reaching the Earth's surface. The result was famine in Iceland and some of the coldest winters on record. More recently, the ash from the 1991 eruption of Mount Pinatubo in the Philippines also affected weather patterns around the world.

IN THE GREENHOUSE

Why is the world heating up?

The most likely explanation seems to be that temperatures are increasing as a result of the greenhouse effect. Heat and light from the sun is vital for life on Earth. But an increase in the levels of some gases in the Earth's atmosphere means that more heat is becoming trapped — just like heat-energy is trapped inside a greenhouse — and more heat-energy means higher temperatures.

LIVING WITH THE RISK

If there is going to be more extreme weather in the future, as many scientists predict, this is bad news for the millions of people who live in flood-risk areas. Bangladesh is one of the poorest and most densely populated countries in the world. Over 80 percent of Bangladeshis live in the countryside and rely on agriculture for a living. Land is essential for their survival, yet the country is at regular risk from cyclones, storm surges and disastrous river floods.

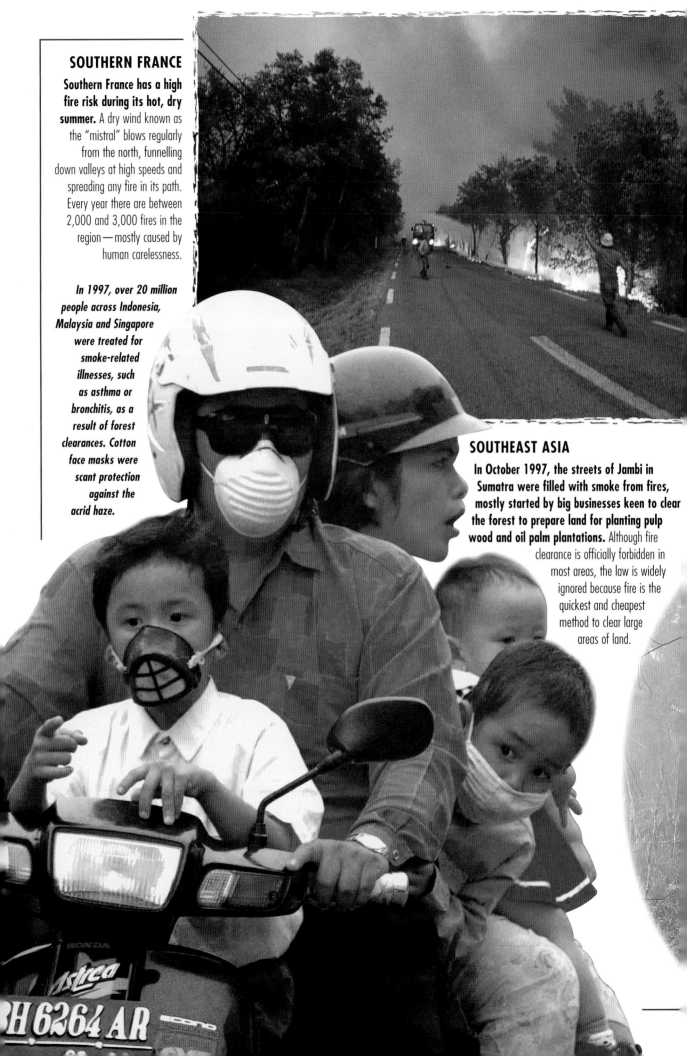

SOUTHERN FRANCE

Southern France has a high fire risk during its hot, dry summer. A dry wind known as the "mistral" blows regularly from the north, funnelling down valleys at high speeds and spreading any fire in its path. Every year there are between 2,000 and 3,000 fires in the region — mostly caused by human carelessness.

In 1997, over 20 million people across Indonesia, Malaysia and Singapore were treated for smoke-related illnesses, such as asthma or bronchitis, as a result of forest clearances. Cotton face masks were scant protection against the acrid haze.

SOUTHEAST ASIA

In October 1997, the streets of Jambi in Sumatra were filled with smoke from fires, mostly started by big businesses keen to clear the forest to prepare land for planting pulp wood and oil palm plantations. Although fire clearance is officially forbidden in most areas, the law is widely ignored because fire is the quickest and cheapest method to clear large areas of land.

HOT SPOTS

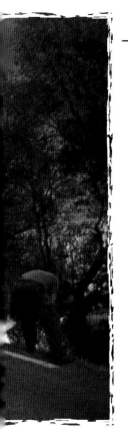

One of the world's hottest spots in 1997 was Southeast Asia. Fires in Indonesia spread a huge cloud of smoke that hung as a thick haze across an area larger than Europe. The worst fires burned in the tropical forests of Sumatra and Kalimantan (the Indonesian part of Borneo). But the smoke affected people across Indonesia, Malaysia, Brunei, and Singapore. Despite predictions of drought, fires started in May and June, and by September they were raging out of control in many places. In the smoke haze from the fires, visibility was so bad that ships ran aground and collided. The smoke even caused a passenger airplane to crash in Sumatra, killing over 200 people. Only when the seasonal rains came in November did the fires finally damp down and the smoke disperse.

WESTERN USA

In 1988 a prolonged drought parched much of the western part of the USA. Following a drought in the previous year, and lower-than-average snowfalls, the fire risk was critical by May of 1988. The first fire in Yellowstone National Park was started by lightning on May 24 and was quickly put out by rain. However, other longer-lasting fires soon followed. By the end of 1988, fire had scorched nearly 800,000 acres (320,000 hectares) of the national park.

SOUTHEAST AUSTRALIA

Eucalyptus trees catch alight very easily because their bark contains highly combustible oils. They also produce lots of litter, which provides excellent dry fuel for a fire. Southeast Australia is one of the most fire-prone regions in the world. During the long summers, hot, dry winds blow in from the desert interior of the continent. Even during the winter, there is usually little rainfall. This means that the environment is usually dry and that fires start and spread very easily.

BURNING FOREST

Amazonia is the largest area of rain forest on Earth, but just as in Indonesia, large companies have been burning vast areas of rain forest as a quick solution to clear areas of land for plantations. Satellite images of South America help scientists to monitor just how fast the rainforest is disappearing. For example, in 1987 it is estimated that over 77, 220 square miles (200,000 square km) of rain forest were destroyed by fire.

FIGHTING A WILDFIRE

ires can cause huge amounts of damage to property and the environment. They can also threaten human life. These threats mean that, in many parts of the world, governments spend many millions of dollars on fire detection and firefighting. Spotting a fire quickly, before it has a chance to take hold and spread, is a priority. Hi-tech equipment, such as infrared scanners mounted in planes, help to pinpoint fires. But in many places the best way to spot a fire is still through human eyes from a fire lookout post. Once the fire has been spotted, firefighters can go into action. Water and foam are sprayed by helicopters and airplanes. Strips of land are bulldozed to act as firebreaks. Planes also drop parachutists, called "smokejumpers," into isolated areas to fight fires.

MAKING A BREAK

A firebreak is a wide corridor that is opened up in a forest. By removing all the trees and other material from the firebreak area, the fire is starved of fuel. Firebreaks make big scars across the landscape, so they are used mainly for big fires.

Firefighters in California spray water from the ground and from the air to try to prevent a fire spreading across a road. Roads, railway tracks, rivers and lakes, and bare rock ledges all act as natural firebreaks. Spraying water on the vegetation on either side of the firebreak makes it less likely that the fire will be able to take hold.

This plane is dumping red retardant on to a forest fire. Retardant is used to slow the advance of a forest fire.

DAMPING DOWN

To put out a fire, firefighters need to remove one of the three essentials for fire: heat, oxygen and fuel. Dumping water on to a fire helps to lower the heat of the fuel. Planes and helicopters are used—some have tanks that are pumped full of water before take-off, others are equipped with scoops so that they can fly over the sea or a lake and refill their tanks with water.

SMOKEJUMPERS

Sometimes the only way in to fight a fire in a remote wilderness area is by air. Firefighters called smokejumpers are dropped in by parachute. Their job is extremely hazardous and requires rigorous training. They have to carry firefighting and survival gear, as well as their parachutes. Often, the firefighters must walk out of the wilderness once the fire is extinguished carrying a backpack weighing up to 110 lb (50 kg).

AFTER A FIRE

Fire has been a regular part of life for plants and animals over millions of years. Many plants have adapted to fire, with bark or leaves that can resist the effects of heat. Others actually rely on fire to make their seeds germinate. Fire can increase the fertility of the soil by releasing nutrients (such as potassium, magnesium, calcium and phosphorus) from the burned vegetation. However, an intense fire can also destroy nutrients in the soil. Faced with fire, animals show little sign of panic but are adept at finding refuges — although a fast-spreading fire will inevitably overwhelm and kill some animals. The biggest threat for most animals is a change in habitat. If an animal relies on only one kind of food, which is destroyed by fire, then that animal may not survive.

TOUGH SEEDS

Some plants, like this Protea, produce seeds with thick outer casings that need the heat of a fire to open them. These seeds can sit in the soil for many years. Only when the outer casing cracks can the seed inside start to germinate and grow.

SEQUOIA SECRETS

Giant sequoias depend on fire to help them flourish. Without fire, other shrubs tend to shade sequoia seedlings and prevent them from growing. A fire will burn competing shrubs, giving the sequoia trees more space and light. The sequoia is well adapted to survive a fire. It has deep roots to avoid damage from a ground fire. Its thick bark protects the living part of the massive trunk from burning, and it has high branches which can escape most fires.

FIRE PINES

Some plants need fire in order to release and germinate their seeds. Many types of pine tree, known as "fire pines," produce seeds that are contained inside closed cones. The cones are held shut by a sticky substance called resin. During a fire, the mature tree may be killed but the cones fall to the ground and the resin melts releasing thousands of seeds on to the newly burned and fertilized soil. "Fire pines" can be found in many countries where there is a risk of fire, like this Lodgepole pine in North America.

BORNEO, 1983
MONKEY SURVIVAL

After massive fires in the rain forests of Borneo in 1983, scientists studied how certain animals adapted to the changed habitat. They noted that a group of macaques quickly changed their pre-fire diet of fruits, seeds and flowers to dried fruits, plants and insects after the fire. Many other small animals make similar adaptations, allowing them to survive in a changed environment after a fire.

YELLOWSTONE SURVIVOR

There are about 30,000 elk in Yellowstone National Park, and about 240 animals perished during the fires of 1988. Most died from the effects of smoke as the fires were swept through the park by strong winds. Many animals, such as bears and bald eagles came into the park straight after the fires to feed on the carcasses of animals killed in the fire.

PREVENTION & SCIENCE: FIRE

YELLOWSTONE, 1988
AN ARGUMENT RAGES

After the Yellowstone fires in 1988, some experts said that the fires would have burned less fiercely, or been prevented altogether, if Yellowstone had been allowed to burn in previous years. They argued that by suppressing fire in the park for many years, fuels had built up to dangerous levels which made the 1988 fires particularly devastating. The balance between allowing fire to take its natural course and keeping fire under control is one that fire experts all over the world have to consider, and the arguments continue to rage.

The best way to stop a fire is never let it start. As we have seen, most environmental fires are started by people, either through carelessness or accidents. Making people more aware of the danger of fire is a big step towards reducing the number of fires, and educating people to deal with fire once it strikes is equally important. Firefighters spray houses with foam to try to protect them from the advance of a forest fire, and foams are also used directly to fight wildfires. They are non-toxic and break down afterwards without harming the environment. Scientists use satellites with infrared (IR) sensors to detect heat, and light sensors to record smoke and other signs of fire. However, clouds block these sensors making them an unreliable source of information. Scientists continue to work on satellite technology for fire detection, but more traditional fire alert systems are more reliable at the present.

EAGLE-EYE VIEW
Fire lookout posts are the main method of fire detection in many places.
Some lookout towers are equipped with TV cameras that scan the landscape below, sending a picture back to a central base. However, it is often difficult to tell the difference between smoke and mist on a TV screen, making the camera lens a less effective fire detector than the human eye. Fire lookout posts are often staffed by volunteers who report any fires to a central control by radio. This one in Oregon is no longer used as a lookout post but has been renovated for use by campers.

FIGHTING FIRE WITH FIRE

Fire can be used itself as a weapon to fight fire. Firefighters sometimes set light to the vegetation that lies in the path of an approaching fire. By controlled burning of a small area they can create a firebreak which starves the main fire of fuel. Fire is also used to prevent possible future fires. This is known as prescribed fire. It is used as part of land management schemes, often to keep fuel levels in check.

SELF-PROTECTION

If you live in a fire-prone area, or you are faced with a wildfire, there is a lot you can do to help yourself. Here are just some of the guidelines issued to people who live in fire risk areas in Australia.

⚫ Fuel reduction is vital: ensure that fallen leaves, long grass and dead undergrowth are regularly cleared away. Clear a firebreak at least 7 feet (2 meters) wide all around your property.

⚫ Make sure you have a good water supply without having to rely on mains water. Keep a supply of water in a tank or in a swimming pool.

⚫ Check your equipment, particularly ladders and hoses. Make sure your hose can reach all sides of the house.

⚫ Prepare for your own personal safety. You will need long-sleeved shirts, and long trousers made from natural fibers (eg. cotton or wool: man-made fibers such as polyester or nylon can melt and burn the skin), sturdy leather boots, gloves, goggles, a wide-rimmed hat.

WET SPOTS

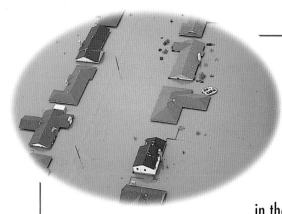

One of the wettest spots on Earth in 1993 was along the Mississippi River in the USA. After a wet spring, thunderstorms brought more rain to the Midwest in the summer — and they stayed. For months the rain fell, making it the wettest summer on record in states such as Minnesota, Illinois and Iowa. Between April and July, Iowa was inundated with as much rain as it usually gets in a whole year. The rainfall swelled the Mississippi River to record levels. The floods started in Minnesota in June, and through the summer they progressed downstream. Towns and farmland along the Mississippi are protected by huge earth banks, called levees, which are designed to contain the river even during a flood. But along the length of the Mississippi the water cascaded over levees more than 20 feet (6 meters) high. Damage to property and farmland was estimated at 10 billion U.S. dollars.

MIGHTY MISSISSIPPI

Floods are a frequent occurrence along the length of the Mississippi but the floods of 1993 were particularly devastating. Many two-storey houses were flooded to the rooftops. The Mississippi is 2,405 miles (3,780 km) long. It runs from Lake Itasca, Minnesota, to the Gulf of Mexico and, together with its tributaries, it drains an area of about 1.2 million square miles (3.2 million square km) including 31 U.S. states and two Canadian provinces.

FLOODED CITY

The beautiful city of Venice in Italy is one of the most unusual in the world. It is built on about 120 small islands in the middle of a lagoon at the north end of the Adriatic Sea. Instead of streets it has canals. Not surprisingly, parts of the city are flooded every year by high tides and storms.

CHINA'S SORROW

The Huang Ho (Yellow River) flows 3,380 miles (5,440 km) from the Himalayas across a vast plain in northern China to the East China Sea. It is known as "China's Sorrow" because, over the centuries, its floods have killed millions of people. For centuries the Chinese have struggled to contain the river by building banks, called dykes, from willow branches, kaoliang (a type of sorghum) stalks, stones, sand, and bricks.

THE LOWLANDS

For over 700 years, the Dutch people have built dykes and dams to stop storm surges flooding their low-lying, marshy coastline. Much of the farmland that lies along the Dutch coast today is land that has been reclaimed from the sea, called polders. This reclaimed land is either at sea level or below it, and needs to be protected by dykes.

FLOODS IN THE DEVELOPING WORLD

People in Dhaka, Bangladesh travel on a wooden boat called a nouka, their umbrellas providing scant protection against the monsoon rains. Floods are the most frequent natural disaster to affect the developing countries of the world. These countries do not have the money to spend on expensive flood protection schemes and many of their floodplains and coastal areas are densely populated. This means that floods and cyclones often have very severe impacts when they strike.

FLOATING HOUSES

The people in the town of Iquitos, Peru, live alongside one of the greatest rivers in the world— the Amazon. Iquitos lies in the shadow of the Andes Mountains, and this part of the river is prone to flooding. But the town of Iquitos rides up and down with the floods. The cane and thatch houses are built on log rafts that sit in a shallow bend of the river.

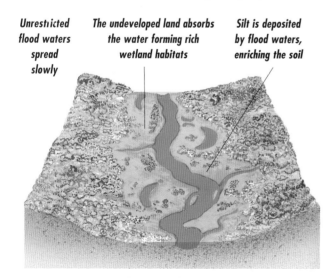

GROWING RICE

Farmers in Bangladesh make the most of the flooding that is part of everyday life in the country. Rice needs water to grow, and it flourishes on the floodplains and deltas of rivers. The seasonal floods in Bangladesh mean that farmers can grow three crops of rice a year. However, severe or unexpected floods can devastate crops, uprooting and damaging plants, and dumping huge amounts of silt in paddy fields.

BUILDING LEVEES

As long as people have lived near rivers, they have built embankments to try to protect themselves from flooding.
In the USA, these embankments are known as levees. The first levee was built along the Mississippi in 1718 to protect the settlement of New Orleans. Since then, the struggle to contain the Mississippi has continued, but levees bring their own problems. They may stop water overflowing in one place, but the extra water can cause worse flooding elsewhere.

Unrestricted flood waters spread slowly

The undeveloped land absorbs the water forming rich wetland habitats

Silt is deposited by flood waters, enriching the soil

Water can push over levees, ruining less protected crops

Levee walls, built to protect towns and crops, can cause flood waters to swell upstream

Fast-flowing waters can breach levees downstream and cause soil erosion

NATURAL FLOODPLAIN

LEVEE-RESTRICTED WATER

LIVING WITH THE THREAT

Some people have always lived with the threat of floods. This is because some of the best agricultural land in the world is found on floodplains. Farmers around the world have long relied on the nutrients deposited by river floods to fertilize the soil. Rivers are also vital links for transport and trade. Over the centuries, as people have settled near rivers, they have also tried to protect themselves from the threat of flood. As long as 2,500 years ago, people in China were building mud banks to try to control the unruly Huang Ho. In Britain, the Romans built floodwalls to protect parts of the coastline. The building of flood barriers, dams and reservoirs continues to this day.

• *See page 86-87 for more information on flood barriers.*

TSUNAMI PROTECTION

Huge concrete slabs form a coastal defense in Japan. Japan has experienced many destructive tsunamis in its history. This type of sea wall helps to absorb the energy of the wave that might otherwise sweep in to destroy buildings.

MOVING HOUSE

Some people who live near the Mississippi have had enough of coping with the river's floods. After the floods in 1993, many communities decided to make a move to safer and higher ground. However, this kind of solution is only available in rich countries, where there is enough wealth to pay for new settlement, and where the population density is not too high — so that there is free land to move to.

AFTER A FLOOD

What happens after the flood waters have gone down, and people start to return to their shattered homes and land?

The first and most devastating consequence of flooding is loss of life. Bodies can be swept far away in a flood; some may never be found. People with injuries need to be evacuated and cared for. Then the clean-up operation can begin. The power of flood waters often smashes houses and washes away foundations. Flood waters also often carry vast amounts of stinking mud which can cover everything in sight once the waters have gone down. Another problem is that flood waters are not clean—the floods run into sewers spreading sewage through houses and streets and increasing the risk of diseases such as cholera, malaria and dysentery.

A woman cleans up after the floods that devastated much of the coast of the Netherlands in 1953. The horrible mess left by flood waters is clear in this picture. Over 70,000 people were evacuated from the area during these floods, and over 400,000 buildings were damaged by the force of the waters.

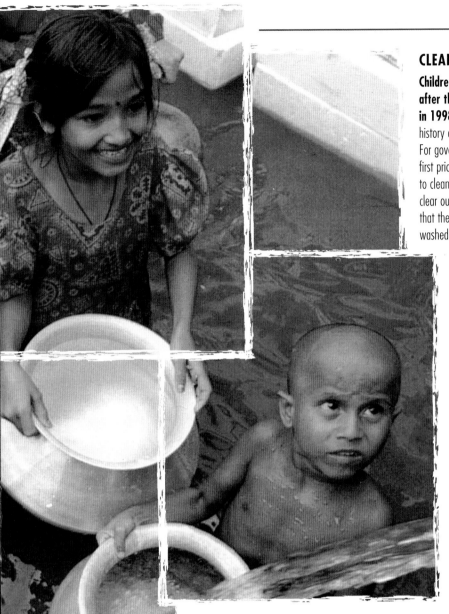

CLEAN WATER

Children collect drinking water from a truck after the floods that hit Dhakar, Bangladesh in 1998. These floods were the worst in the history of Bangladesh and left millions homeless. For governments and aid agencies, one of the first priorities is to ensure that people have access to clean water supplies. The next priority is to clear out and clean up wells, and make sure that they are not contaminated by sewage washed in by the flood waters.

HONDURAS, 1998

The capital of Honduras, Tegucigalpa, was devastated by floods caused by Hurricane Mitch as up to 4 inches (10 cm) of rain fell per hour at the height of the storm. An eyewitness described her helplessness as..."several neighbours' homes [were] washed away in the storm. The house below ours filled with mud to the eaves. We moved out of our house...when the bank below us began to crumble away...Many of those who rescued others had themselves watched their own homes flooded or jerked away by the currents..."

RUINED CROPS

Farmers stand in the ruins of their fields in Honduras surveying the devastation caused by Hurricane Mitch in 1998. The hurricane winds shredded vegetation, and torrential rain caused massive mudslides and floods. Over half of all the crops in Honduras were destroyed by the storm. Aid agencies provided food relief for over half a million people who were in danger of starvation. Another priority was to distribute seeds, so that fields could be cleared and replanted in good time to provide crops for the next season.

ART RESCUE

"The Arno is out!" This was the cry around Florence, Italy, on the night of November 4, 1966. After very heavy rain, the River Arno finally flooded the historic city. The floods rose to 20 feet (6 meters), causing extensive damage to many important historical buildings, artwork and sculptures. One of the main problems was the oil that leaked out of central heating units and coated everything it touched. In the library, more than a million books were covered in thick, oily mud, some dating from Renaissance times. Volunteers were forced to wear gas masks to guard against the stink of sewage and rotting leather. Experts searched the mud for tiny fragments of damaged frescoes, and cleaned and restored paintings. The huge international effort helped to rescue many priceless works of art.

PREVENTION & SCIENCE: FLOODS

What precautions can be taken against floods and what scientific advances give hope for the future? Today, meteorologists and hydrologists make use of the latest, hi-tech equipment to monitor water flows and rainfall. Scientists can now obtain accurate information from rain gauges mounted in aircraft or on satellites. Weather radar is also used, and combined with information from ground gauges, readings can be given for whole areas. All this information is processed by computers. To control rivers and protect coastlines, the wealthy, developed nations often have extensive and complicated systems of dams, reservoirs, dykes and barrages—although even the most hi-tech schemes may fail in the event of a "super flood."
• See page 54-55 for more information on dams.

WATCHING FOR WAVES

After the tsunami that hit Hawaii in 1946, it was decided to set up a warning system in the Pacific region. This system is now known as the Tsunami Warning System, and 26 nations work together to collect data and issue warnings. This system makes use of satellites and sensors right across the Pacific region which alert weather offices if a tsunami is on its way. However, warnings of tsunamis do not, sometimes, have the desired effect. After warning of a tsunami in 1964, thousands of people flooded on to the beaches of San Francisco to watch!

VENICE IN PERIL

In 1996, St Mark's Square in Venice was flooded for 101 days. This was the worst year on record. Venice is threatened by two main problems: rising sea levels as a result of global warming, and the fact that Venice itself is sinking. For years, scientists and politicians have been arguing about the best way to protect Venice. One plan is called the Moses Project. It would involve fixing 79 hinged barriers to the sea bed at the mouth of the lagoon. These barriers would be raised in the event of a higher than normal tide. However, many people are concerned about the effect of a barrier on wildlife in the lagoon. Another problem with a barrier, as with all coastal defenses, is that the water it deflects could cause worse flooding further along the coast.

HOW THE BARRIERS WOULD WORK?

The barriers would remain on the sea bed until the tide is 3 feet higher than normal.

To raise the barriers, compressed air would pump out the water and the barriers would float to the surface.

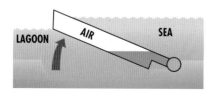

WATER

LAGOON   AIR   SEA

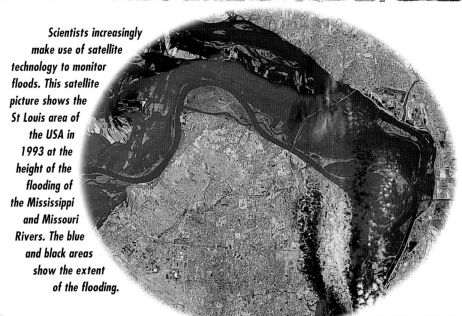

Scientists increasingly make use of satellite technology to monitor floods. This satellite picture shows the St Louis area of the USA in 1993 at the height of the flooding of the Mississippi and Missouri Rivers. The blue and black areas show the extent of the flooding.

HI-TECH BARRIERS

Many countries have invested in hi-tech solutions to protect important places from flooding. Since 1983, London, UK has been protected from a storm surge, such as the one that hit eastern England in 1953, by the Thames Barrier. Normally the barrier lies flat on the riverbed. But if warning of a storm surge is received, the gates are raised so that they stand 52 feet (16 meters) above the riverbed. It takes about 30 minutes to raise the gates completely.

FLOOD MYTHS

Myths about floods are found in cultures all over the world.

In these stories, a flood is often sent by the gods to punish wicked people on Earth. In the Bible story of Noah, the Ark contains two of every bird and animal as well as Noah's family. The Ancient Babylonians told the story of Enlil who sent a great flood to quieten the peoples of the world. The Hindu story of Manu relates that Manu was warned by a fish to build a ship. When the floods came, the fish pulled the ship and Manu to safety.

The Aztec people of Central America believed that in the past, the world had been destroyed by both fire and flood. This statue is of the Aztec raingod Tlaloc. Both the Aztecs and the Incas of South America also worshipped fire gods.

UNCOVERING THE PAST

There have been fires and floods as long as humans have been living on Earth. Ancient peoples told powerful stories, called myths, to try to explain these terrifying natural phenomena. Scientists today know about some ancient fires and floods from archaeological deposits and remains. A layer of clay and debris deep in the ground can indicate a flood thousands of years ago. A layer of charcoal can indicate an ancient fire and can be dated quite precisely. Trees can also reveal useful information. Both floods and fires can leave scars on a tree, which show up in the tree's growth rings. These scars can be used to date floods and fires, a technique known as dendrochronology.

THE PHOENIX

The story of the Phoenix comes from Greek mythology. Some writers relate that this brightly colored bird lived for 500 years, some that it lived for up to 12,954 years. At the time of its death, it burned itself on a pyre of spice tree twigs. Then a new Phoenix rose from the ashes with renewed youth and beauty. The young Phoenix took the ashes of its father to the city of Heliopolis in Egypt, the City of the Sun.

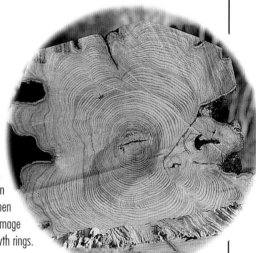

DENDROCHRONOLOGY

The growth rings in a tree may tell the story of a fire or flood. In the year of a fire the ring may be narrower, but in following years the rings are often wider than average because of the added nutrients in the soil as result of the fire. A flood can damage a tree when debris carried in the waters crashes into a tree, injuring the living wood beneath the bark. This damage shows up in the growth rings.

ANCIENT FLOOD

Some of the earliest-known civilizations on Earth were on the floodplains of the Tigris and Euphrates Rivers in an area known as Mesopotamia (modern-day Iraq). The peoples of this area must have experienced many floods. In 1929, excavations at the ancient city of Ur uncovered a thick layer of clay deep under the ground. This 10-foot (3-m) layer indicated that many thousands of years ago there had been a massive flood, probably up to 25 feet (7.5 meters) deep.

IRAQ, 1929
NOAH'S FLOOD

The archaeologist in charge of the excavation at the ancient city of Ur was a British man, Sir Leonard Woolley. After examining the thick layer of clay flood deposits he wrote, "We had thus found the flood on which is based the story of Noah." For the ancient people caught in this flood, it must have seemed as if the deluge covered the whole Earth.

GLOSSARY

Beaufort scale
The scale used to judge wind speed. See also the glossary entry on hurricanes.

category (of hurricanes)
The Saffir-Simpson scale used to judge hurricane intensity. The most severe hurricanes are category-5, with a wind speed of over 155 mph (250 km/h.)

crust
The layer of solid rock between the earth's surface and its molten interior.

cyclone
A severe tropical storm occurring in the Indian ocean.

dam
A barrier built to hold back water. The water is then used as a reservoir or to make electricity.

dyke
A wall built to prevent flooding.

epicenter
The point on the earth's surface directly above an earthquake.

erupt
A volcano which releases lava, gases and ashes.

extinct volcano
A volcano which it is believed will not erupt again.

firebreak
An area of land cleared of all material that can burn. Without fuel, a fire cannot cross a firebreak and so it is prevented from spreading.

flash flood
A sudden flood.

floodplain
An area of low lying ground near a river that is regularly flooded.

GMT
Greenwich Mean Time. A standard way of measuring time. It is based on the time at Greenwich in London, England.

global warming
An increase in the earth's temperature caused by pollution in the atmosphere.

hurricane
A severe storm of force 12 on the Beaufort scale. Wind speed is above 74 mph (119 km/h.)

lava
Molten rock released from a volcano.

levee
A bank of earth built to prevent flooding.

magma
The liquid rocks inside the earth's crust.

GLOSSARY

magnitude (of earthquakes)
The Richter scale used to judge the severity of earthqukes. A magnitude 5 earthquake causes slight damage. A magnitude 8 earthquake is devastating. Each point on the scale represents an earthquake 10 times as powerful, so magnitude 8 is 1,000 times more powerful than magnitude 5.

meteorologists
Scientists who study the weather.

molten rocks
Rocks that have been turned to a liquid by intense heat.

monsoon
The seasonal winds that affect the weather in southeast Asia: hot, dry weather in the summer and severe rains in winter.

Richter scale
The scale used to judge the severity of earthqukes (see the glossary entry for magnitude.)

Ring of Fire
The area at the edge of the Pacific ocean which is particularly prone to earthquakes and volcanoes.

seismic activity
The vibrations in the earth caused by an earthquake.

seismologists
Scientists who study earthquakes.

tectonic plate
The huge plates that the world's oceans and landmasses rest upon. The movement of tectonic plates causes earthquakes and volcanoes.

tornado
Strong, swirling winds that look like a funnel from the sky, moving along the ground.

tremor
Small vibrations in the earth, which often occur before an earthquake.

tsunami
A huge wave caused by an earthquake under the sea.

twister
Another name for a tornado.

typhoon
A severe tropical storm occurring in the Pacific ocean.

volcanologists
Scientists who study volcanoes.

waterspout
Swirling winds containing water and spray, which occurs when a tornado forms over water.

whirlwind
Another name for a tornado.

INDEX

A

aa (lava) 22
Abu Simbel 54
Achilles 13
agriculture 97, 116, 117
Aguán river, Honduras 71
air pollution 105
Akrotiri, Thira 15, 37
Alaska 7, 29, 44, 50
Amazon River 116
Amazonia 107
Anchorage, Alaska 44
Andes Mountains 31, 40, 52, 53
andesite 31
animals *see* wildlife
Arafura Sea 78
archaeology 36-7, 122-3
Aristotle 12, 40
Armero, Colombia 26
Arriola, Laura 71
Arsia, Mars 39
Ascraeus Mons, Mars 39
ash 18, 19, 25
Aswan Dam, Egypt 54, 96
Atlantic Ocean 68, 70-1, 93
atmospheric pressure 89
atolls 33
Australia 73, 82, 83, 92, 98, 104, 107
Aztecs 56, 122

B

Bahamas 70
Bali 29, 33
Bangladesh 69, 74-5, 95, 96, 104, 105, 115, 116, 119
barographs 89
barometers 89
barrages 120
basalt 31
Beaufort, Sir Francis 90
Beaufort scale 90
Bermuda Triangle 84
Besakih temple 29
Black Dragon (Amur) River, China 98
black sand/lava 33
body waves 45
Borneo 111
Bosch, Hieronymus 12
brimstone (sulfur) 12
Brunei 107
Building Research Institute 65

Buriganga River, Bangladesh 74
bushfires 98, 104

C

calderas 19, 32
California, USA 10, 42, 62, 63, 64
campfires 99
Canary Islands 28
Cape Mendocino, California 43
Cappadocia, Turkey 31
carbon dioxide 25
Caribbean Sea 25, 70
Casitas volcano, Nicaragua 76
Causeway Bay, Hong Kong 72
Cerro Negro volcano, Nicaragua 76
CFCs (chlorofluorcarbons) 91
Chance, Mount, Montserrat 25
Chang Heng 47
Charles Heddles (ship) 74
Chile 46, 50
China 53, 62, 98, 104, 114, 117
climate 91
Cocos Plate 56
Colombia 26
Colorado, USA 54, 55, 56
Colossus 60, 61
Comoro Islands 75
Conrad, Joseph 73
copper 31
corals 33
Crater Lake, Oregon 32
craters 14, 19, 32, 33
    see also calderas
creepmeters 63
Crete 14, 37
crop circles 84
crust *see* Earth
currents 92
cyclones 69, 73, 74-5, 78-9, 96
Cyprus 61

D

dams 54, 55, 86, 96, 101, 120
Darwin, Australia 78-9
dendrochronology 123
Denver, Colorado 54
Dhaka, Bangladesh 74, 115, 119
Diamond Hill, Honolulu 32
diamonds 31

Disaster Prevention Day 58
disasters 26-7, 57, 94-5
drought 104
dust devils 83
dykes 19, 115, 120

E

Earth
    core 16
    crust 16, 19, 30, 40
    mantle 16, 19, 40
earthquake-resistant
    buildings 64
earthquakes 8-9, 20, 26-27, 40-65
    causes 41
    and floods 101
    man-made 54-5
    measuring 35
    precautions 64-5
    predicting 62-3
    research 64-5
    Alaska, 1964 44
    ancient 60-1
    Chile 48, 50
    Japan 58-9
    Kazakhstan 52
    Lisbon 48, 49, 97
    Maharashtra 52
    Mexico City 56-7
    San Francisco 42-3, 45
Easter Island 50
Egypt 54, 96, 123
ejecta 25, 39
embankments 116
epicenter 44
eruptions, effects 26-7
Etna, Mount, Sicily 12, 13, 18, 20, 73
Eurasian Plate 58
Europe 82
extrusive rocks 30, 31
"eye," storm 69

F

fault lines 10-11
fertilization of soil 96, 117
Finn Mac Cool 31
fires 96-9, 104, 106, 108-9, 123
    effects 110-11
    fighting 108-9, 112-13
    forest clearance 97, 106,

107
    warning signs 102, 103
fishing 90, 93
fissure eruptions 31
fissures 20
Flood Action Plan 74
flood barriers 74, 86, 87, 117
floods 69, 91, 96-7, 100-1, 104, 114-15
    aftermath 118-19
    living with 116-17
    myths 122-3
    prevention 120-1
    warning signs 102
    Bangladesh 74-5
Florence, Italy 119
Florida, USA 68, 70, 76, 77
focus (hypocenter) 44, 45
Fox Point Hurricane Dam 86
France 31, 106
Fugen, Mount, Japan 24
Fujita scale 80
Fujita, T. Theodore 80
fumaroles 8, 19, 20

G

Gaia 73
Gakukei space probe 39
Galapagos 23, 28, 34
Galileo Galilei 38
Galveston, Texas 66
Ganges delta 69
gases 19, 20, 22, 25
    see also sulfur
geological survey stations 63
geothermal power 34
Giant's Causeway, Northern Ireland 31
glacier flood 7
global warming 91, 104, 105, 120
gold 31
Golden, Colorado 56
Golunggung, Indonesia 25
granite 30, 45
Great Rift Valley 11, 32
Greek fire 12
Greek mythology 123
"greenhouse gases" 91, 105
Grimsvötn, Iceland 7
groundwater 62, 63
Gunung Agung, Bali 29

INDEX

H

Hawaii, USA 12, 16, 17, 23, 51
Hedditch, Bob 78
Heimaey, Iceland 27
Helgafell, Iceland 27
Heliopolis, Egypt 123
Helios, sun god 61
Hephaistos (Vulcanus) 13
Herculaneum 15, 18, 26, 60
Hernandez, Gabriel and Maria
    Isabel 87
Hina-Ai-Malama (Pele),
    Polynesian goddess 12
Hinggan forest, China 98
Hiroshige, Ando 67
Hollywood, USA 72
Honduras 71, 76, 104, 119
Hong Kong 72
Honolulu 32
Honshu, Japan 58-9
Hoover Dam 54
Huang Ho (Yellow River), China
    114, 117
Huascaran, Mount 52, 53
Hurricane (film) 72
hurricanes 66-95
    Atlantic 68, 70-1
    and El Niño 92
    intensity scale 71
    names 67
    precautions 86
    tracking 85, 102
    warnings 88
    zones 69
    Alicia 66
    Andrew 70, 76, 77, 94, 102
    Camille 76
    Fran 67
    Georges 68, 70
    Gilbert 104
    Katrina 70
    Mitch 70, 71, 76, 104, 119
    Pauline 92
    Rita 70
    see also typhoons
hydrological cycle 102
hypocenter (focus) 44, 45

I

Iceland 7, 10, 18, 27
igneous rocks 30
Imperial Valley, California 43
Incas 92, 122

India 52, 83
Indian Ocean 69, 74-5
Indonesia 14, 25, 29, 87, 92,
    107
International Union for Geological
    Sciences 52
intrusive rocks 30
Io 38, 39
Iquitos, Peru 116

J

Jambi, Sumatra 106
Japan 24, 26, 35, 51, 58-9,
    63, 73, 117
Jarrell, Texas 87
jökulhlaup (glacier flood) 7
Jupiter 38, 39

K

Kalimantan, Indonesia 107
Kamchatka 24
Kansas 82
Kant, Immanuel 49
Kariba Dam 55
Kashmir 52
Katrina 70
Knossos, Crete 60
Kobe, Japan 58, 59
Kodiak, Alaska 50
Krafla field, Iceland 18
Krakatoa 14, 22, 23, 24, 29
Kublai Khan 73
Kutso reservoir, Lesotho 54
Kyushu, Japan 73

L

Labor Day 1935 77
Laetoli, Tanzania 36
lahars (mudslides) 26
Lamour, Dorothy 72
landslides 40, 52-3, 101
lapilli 25
laser technology 62
lava 15, 17, 22, 26
lava flows 22, 27
Le Puy, France 31
Lesotho 54
levees 70, 116
lightning 98
Lisbon earthquake 48, 49, 97
Los Angeles, USA 43
Love waves 45
Lynmouth, Devon 100

M

McKinley, William 88
Magellan space probe 38
magma 16, 17, 19, 20, 30
magnetometers 63
Maharashtra, India 52
Malaysia 107
Maldives, Indian Ocean 87
Mandraki, Rhodes 61
mantle see Earth
Manu 122
Mars 38, 39
Martinique 15, 24, 33
Mauna Loa, Hawaii 17
Mausoleum 60
Mayotte, Comoro Islands 75
Mazama, Mount 32
Mercalli, Giuseppe 47
meteorology 95, 102
meteosats (meteorological
    satellites) 89
Mexico, Gulf of 70, 82
Mexico City 56-7
Michoacan, Mexico 56
Milne, John 47
Mindanao, Philippines 87
Mississippi River 114, 117, 121
"mistral" 106
Moluccas, Indonesia 87
monsoons 100, 115
Montserrat, Caribbean 25
Moon 38
Morris, Neil 76
Moses Project 120
Mount see Etna; St Helens etc
mudflows 52-3
mudslides 26, 29, 76
mushroom clouds 25

N

namazu 58
Namibia 41
NAO (North Atlantic Oscillation) 93
Naples, Italy 18
Nasser, Lake 54
National Earthquake Information
    Center (U.S.) 56
National Hurricane Center (U.S.)
    76, 77
National Meteorological Center
    (U.S.) 103
National Severe Storms
    Laboratory (U.S.) 82

National Weather Service 103
Nazco Oceanic Plate 40
Nebraska, USA 82
Netherlands 101, 115, 118
Nevada del Ruiz, Colombia 26
New Guinea 73
New Orleans, USA 70
New Zealand 20
Ngorongoro Crater, Tanzania 32
Nicaragua 50, 51, 70, 76
Nile, River 54, 96
El Niño 92-3, 95
NOAA (National Oceanic and
    Atmospheric Administration)
    103
Noah's ark 122, 123
North America 82, 92
    see also named places
North American Plate 56, 58
Northridge, California 42
Novarupta, Alaska 29
nuclear explosions 54

O

obsidian 31
Oklahoma, USA 82
Olympia 61
Olympus Mons, Mars 39
Oplontis 15
Osaka, Japan 58
ozone hole 91

P

"P" (primary) waves 45
Pacific Ocean 31, 43, 56, 68,
    72, 73
Pacific Plate 43, 58
Pacific Tsunami Warning Center,
    Hawaii 51
pahoehoe (lava flow) 22
Pakistan 52
Papua New Guinea 28
Parkfield, California 63
Pavonis, Mars 39
Pele (Hina-Ai-Malama),
    Polynesian goddess 12
Pelée, Mont 15, 24
Peléean eruptions 23
Peru 52, 53, 93, 116
Pharos 60
Philippine Plate 58
Philippines 27, 105
Phoenix 123

INDEX

Piddington, Henry 74
Pinatubo, Mount, Philippines 27, 105
plants 29, 110-11
plate movements 8-9, 34, 40, 41
Plinian eruptions 23, 25
Pliny 14
polar ice sheets 104
polders 115
Pompeii 15, 36-7, 60
Poseidon 60
Preston, Robert 72
Priya (Indian baby) 52
pumice 31
pyroclastic flows 24, 25

R
Rabaul, Papua New Guinea 28
radiometers 95
rain 85, 92, 102, 103
rain gauges 103
Rainier, Mount USA 7
Rangely, Colorado, USA 55
Rayleigh waves 45
relief agencies 74
rescue services 53
research 64-5, 94
reservoirs 120
Resina 18
Richter, Charles Francis 46
Richter scale 46, 47
"Ring of Fire" 8-9 31, 56
Rita (hurricane) 70
rocks 30-1, 41
Roraima (ship) 24

S
"S" (secondary) waves 45
safety precautions 86-7
Saffir, Herbert 71
Saffir-Simpson scale 71
Sahara Desert 83
St Elmo's Fire 22
St Helens, Mount, USA 20, 21, 23, 28
St Louis, USA 121
St Pierre, Martinique 15, 24
San Andreas Fault 42-3, 63
San Francisco, USA 6, 42, 43, 45, 65, 120
San Juan del Sur, Nicaragua 50
sandstone 45

Santa Cruz mountains 45
Santorini (Thira) 14
Sapas Mons, Venus 38
satellites 88, 89, 94, 121
Scott, Ellery 24
sea levels 104, 120
sea walls 87
seaquakes 50
seismic activity 20
seismic waves 44-5
seismograms 46
seismographs 35, 46-7
Seismological Society 47
seismology 63, 64-5
seismometers 47, 63
sequoias 110
shifting cultivation 97
shock absorbers 64
Sicily 18
sills, volcanic 19
silver 31
smoke risks 106, 107
"smokejumpers" 108, 109
snakes 20
South America 92
    see also named places
South American Continental Plate 40
South Pacific 33
spontaneous combustion 98
Stabiae 14, 15
stilt houses 87
storm cellars 87
storm chasers 80, 84
storm surges 69, 86, 87, 96, 101, 115
storms 76-7, 91
strainmeters 63
strata 41
Stromboli 20
Strombolian eruptions 23
subduction 41
sulfur 20, 22, 25, 33, 39
Sumatra 50, 106, 107
Sumbawa island, Indonesia 14
surface waves 45
survival kits 65

T
Tambora, Mount 14
Tangshan 62
Tanzania 36
Tartarus 73

Tay Bridge, Scotland 80
Tegucigalpa, Honduras 119
Texas, USA 82, 83, 87
Thames Barrier 121
thermocouples, 34
Thira (Santorini) 14, 15, 33, 37
tidal waves see tsunamis
Tlaloc 122
Tokyo, Japan 58
Tolbachik, Mount, Kamchatka 24
TOPEX/Poseidon satellites 95
tornado alley 82-3, 87
tornadoes 80-1, 85, 86, 87, 92
Torricelli, Evangelista 89
TOTO (Totable Tornado Observatory) 82
trade winds 69, 91, 92
tremors 20, 35, 54
tropical storms see cyclones; hurricanes; typhoons
tropics 68-9
Truman, Harry 20
Tsunami Warning System 120
tsunamis 26, 44, 50-1, 100, 117, 120
Turkey 31
Twister (film) 84
twisters 82, 83
Typhoeus (Typhon) 73
Typhoon (Conrad) 73
Typhoon (film) 72
typhoons 68, 73, 77, 87
    see also hurricanes

U
Ur 123
U.S. Geological Survey 64

V
Vaiont Dam, Italy 101
Varanasi, India 100
Venezuela 90
Venice, Italy 114, 120
vents 19, 20
Venus 38
Vestmannaeyjar, Iceland 27
Vesuvius, Mount 14, 15, 18, 21, 26, 37, 60
volcanic activity, and floods 101
volcanic mud 33
volcanic pollution 105
volcanic soil 28

volcanoes 8-9, 12-39
    active 15
    beneficial results 28-9
    blowing 23
    causes 41
    cross-section 19
    effect on weather 105
    extinct 15, 33
    health hazards 27
    inactive 33
    space 38-9
    submarine 33
    warning signs 20-1
volcanology 34-5
Voltaire 48
Voyager space probes 39
Vulcan (Vulcanus; Hephaistos) 13
Vulcanian eruptions 23

W
Waco, Texas, USA 83
water cycle 102
water pressure 55
waterspouts 80, 81, 84, 85
Watson, W.J. 22
weather 91, 104-5
    forecasting 102
Weather Forecast Offices 103
weather planes 88
weather radar 120
weather stations 88-9, 94
Wegener, Alfred 12
wetlands 116
whirlwinds 85
    see also tornadoes
White Island, New Zealand 20
wildlife (animals) 28-9, 34, 49, 85, 96, 110-11
winds 73, 84, 85, 102, 106
    trade 69, 91, 92
World Meteorological Organization 67

Y
Yellow River, China 114, 117
Yellowstone National Park, USA 107, 111, 112
Yokohama 58, 59
Yungay, Peru 52

Z
Zambezi River 55
Zeus 60, 61